AS "JUST RIGHT" BUSINESS QUESTIONS

ASKING "JUST RIGHT" BUSINESS QUESTIONS

A Proven Process For Developing Leaders And Organizations

Curtis W. Page, Ph.D. & Charles J. Selden

Revised Edition

Published By:

The Graham Page

Copyright © 1994 by Curtis W. Page, Ph.D. and Charles J. Selden

All rights reserved. No part of this book may be reproduced or transmitted in any form or by any means, electronic or mechanical, including photocopying recording, or by any information storage and retrieval system, without permission in writing from the publisher.

Published by The Graham Page
5540-38 West Fifth Street
Oxnard, California 93035

Books may be purchased for educational, business or seminar use. For information call: 1-800-272-3617

Printed in the United States of America

Library of Congress Catalog Card Number: 94-76163

ISBN 1-885207-00-X

Revised Edition

ABOUT THE AUTHORS

Curtis W. Page, Ph.D., is Professor of Behavioral Science/Organizational Behavior, School of Business and Management, Pepperdine University, Malibu, California.

Dr. Page is actively consulting with Fortune 100 companies, and was a major contributor to the design and implementation of the Presidential Key Executive (PKE) MBA Program and the Technology Management Master of Science Degree Program at Pepperdine. He is a Licensed Psychologist, State of California and has written several books on business and organization management. He resides with his wife in the Los Angeles area.

Charles J. Selden is CEO of Full Perspective Video Services, an Indiana-based firm specializing in the marketing and distribution of special interest videos. Previously, he was a publisher of educational materials at Random House. He has an MBA from Pepperdine, an MA in Communications from Stanford, and an MA in English and Creative Writing from the University of Iowa. Mr. Selden lives in the New York City metropolitan area with his wife and son.

DEDICATION

This effort of mine can only be dedicated to Elsie Marie Page, my wife and associate. Her loving support over many years has assured the energies to gain the experiences that have culminated in this book.

Acknowledgment is extended to (1) all of my graduate students at Pepperdine University over the past twenty-five years for the myriad "just right" questions about every facet of business, (2) my colleagues on the faculty of the School of Business and Management with whom I have discussed those questions, and (3) my public and private sector clients over the years for the privilege of having the challenges of repeated experiences where the "just right" questions could be tested again and again.

Finally, there is a special feeling of gratitude and appreciation that must be expressed to my friend and co-author, Charles Selden . He has made this book a reality through his knowledge, perseverance, and writing capability. His humor helped, too.

Curtis W. Page
San Pedro, 1994

This book is for my lovely wife, Patricia, who is too wise to ask too many questions and for my handsome son, Kurt, who is now wise enough to seek answers.

I would like to acknowledge the following: Watching Duke Page ask questions of executives who thought they had all the answers—before they heard some of the questions, that is—was how the idea got started.

Long ago I was lucky enough to study under Professor John Dando at Trinity College. He sensitized me to the just right word and I have never been the same since.

Charles Selden
Montclair, 1994

Table of Contents

PROLOGUE

Questions First, Answers Later 1
THERE ARE NO READY-MADE ANSWERS 1
THE ANATOMY OF ASKING QUESTIONS 8
THE QUESTIONING MINDSET 12
USING THIS BOOK 15
THE QUESTIONS LIST
    SEEING 17
    AIMING 17
    DOING 17

Chapter 1

SEEING 19

WHAT BUSINESS ARE WE REALLY IN? 20
WHAT IS OUR IDENTITY? 23
ARE WE INNOVATORS OR AUGMENTORS? 26
WHAT ARE OUR RESOURCES? 30
WHAT ARE OUR ASSUMPTIONS? 33
HOW DOES THE FUTURE LOOK? 36
WHAT RISKS SHOULD WE TAKE? 40
HOW DO WE DEVELOP OUR GOAL? 44
WHAT ARE OUR THINKING PATTERNS? 48
WHAT ARE OUR ALTERNATIVES? 52
WHAT ABOUT STARTING OVER? 55

Chapter 2
AIMING 59

WHAT IS OUR STRATEGY? 60
WHAT DO WE WANT TO HAPPEN? 64
WHAT IS OUR ORGANIZING PRINCIPLE? 68
WHAT IS OUR COMPLEXITY LEVEL? 71
WHAT SEGMENTS ARE WE SEEKING? 75
WHAT IS THE ATTRACTION? 78
WHAT ARE OUR RESOURCE ORIGINS? 81
WHAT ARE THE TRENDS? 84
HOW CONDUCIVE ARE THE CONDITIONS? 87
WHAT SPECIAL FACTORS INFLUENCE OUR
    BUSINESS ENVIRONMENT? 90
WHAT CONSEQUENCES ARE WE SETTING IN
    MOTION? 94
WHO ARE OUR AUDIENCES? 98
WHAT ARE THE READINESS LEVELS? 100
WHAT IS THE PROCESS FOR OBJECTIVES
    EVALUATION? 103
WHAT ARE OUR STRATEGIC OPTIONS ? 106

Chapter 3
DOING 111

WHAT ARE OUR TACTICS? 112
WHERE ARE THE BOTTLENECKS? 115
WHAT KINDS OF MANAGERS DO WE NEED? 118
HOW DO WE MAINTAIN CONTROL? 122
HOW DO WE ACHIEVE POWER INTEGRATION? .. 126
HOW DO WE STAY IN THE HERE-AND-NOW? 130
WHAT IS REALLY GOING ON? 133

HOW DOES OUR COMMUNICATION OF
    OBJECTIVES TAKE PLACE 136
HOW WILL WE SECURE COMMITMENT? 140
HOW DO WE HANDLE ROLE EXPECTATIONS? 144
HOW DO WE ACHIEVE PRODUCTIVITY? 147
HOW DO WE GET FEEDBACK 150
HOW ARE WE MANAGING OUR RESOURCE
    BASE? 154
HOW DO WE ACCOMPLISH DECISION
    IMPLEMENTATION? 157
WHAT IS THE COMMONALITY? 161
HOW DO WE DESIGN USEFUL MEASUREMENT
    OF RESULTS? 164
HOW EFFECTIVE AND EFFICIENT IS OUR
    OPERATION? 167
WHAT ARE THE CHANGE INDICATORS? 170

EPILOGUE

The Road To Implementation 173
WHAT DO WE DO WITH OUR ANSWERS 173
WHO WILL CHAMPION THE CAUSE? 176

Additional Reading Suggestions 178
HOW SHOULD WE BE READING? 178
WHAT BOOKS AND ARTICLES MIGHT
    STIMULATE JUST RIGHT QUESTIONS? 180

Index 184

PROLOGUE

Questions First, Answers Later

THERE ARE NO READY-MADE ANSWERS

The Maze of Problems and Opportunities

Propelled by technology, fueled by economics, influenced by politics, and subjected to cultural values, *change* is the most common problem with which managers and leaders continually grapple.

Change occurs with the speed of a trend switch in the Dow Jones Industrial Averages. Or it creeps in like rust on inadequately serviced equipment. It surprises us with the emergence of a hot new company with an innovative new product or amazes us with the sudden demise of a once invincible company where fresh ideas went stale.

Change thrusts problems upon us and then pressures us for solutions that must be found quickly if we and our organizations are to prosper. It is clear we need to find answers. *But before there can be useful answers, there must be penetrating questions.* The questions must be "just right" because the world is changing so rapidly. Trying to make someone else's answer fit our needs fails because the circumstances originally leading up to that answer were different from ours. Answers emerge when we deal with problems in the present. Not when we look for them in a past no longer resembling the present.

In the 1980's, organizations as different as Apple Computer, the public broadcasting television stations, and the U.S. auto industry were confronted by the need to find answers to fundamental problems brought on by change. The changes were not very different from the sort faced by you and your organization: The questions come from market shifts, regulation changes, new opportunities, and technological breakthroughs. The questions

ASKING "JUST RIGHT" BUSINESS QUESTIONS

have application to you and your organization as well. The answers you come up with will be different from these industries and companies, but the answers will more likely fit your needs and meet the challenges of your problems.

The Worm in the Core: Apple Computer

Apple was the envy of its technological competition. In the forefront of the home microcomputer revolution, Steven Jobs and Steve Wozniak, Apple's founding fathers, saw the possibilities for personal computers when giants like IBM were concentrating on computers for commercial use. Jobs and Wozniak's strategy was to build reliable and affordable computers. They worried traditionalists by the way they organized Apple Computer. It was informal, emphasized engineering, and attracted people who thrived in start-up situations.

As the business and markets grew, new problems arose requiring a different kind of thinking from the sort that had made them so successful so quickly. Apple's problem was being on the forefront of innovation—and getting too close to it. There was the inevitable shakeout: Computer outlets started drying up and therefore Apple Computer's manufacturing capacity had to be curtailed. To ensure Apple's survival, the emphasis was switched from engineering to marketing. Wozniak quietly left to form another company and Jobs noisily left as a result of a boardroom squeeze play.

How should growth be sustained?

How can emerging competition be met?

Jobs' removal was engineered by John Sculley, a marketing whiz originally brought to Apple by Jobs. Sculley, who, in turn, left in 1993, saw the opportunities for Apple in an environment markedly different from the one in which Apple began. Sculley's people could have asked these questions about what to do next:

What have been our assumptions?

How does the future look?

What are our alternatives?

· PROLOGUE ·

Lost and Found Funding: Public Broadcasting Stations

In the 1960s public broadcasting stations could count on a constant flow of federal funds and generous support from corporations with deep pockets and a keen desire for a positive image. In the 1970s, as the American economy slowed, perceptions of public broadcasting changed. The national mood was less generous because national resources were pressured by other demands. Congress, formerly a supportive parent, felt it had raised a child whose time had come to be more self-sustaining. The PBS stations, once focused only on what to do with their money, now had to ask where to find it.

Each affiliate needed to find answers by asking questions:

What is our strategy in an altered environment?

Who are our audiences and how can we broaden the base?

What are our alternatives?

Time for a Tune-up: The U.S. Auto Industry

Detroit was once the world center for automobile design, manufacturing, and marketing. In 1950 General Motors, Ford, and the Chrysler Corporation were the "Big Three" of worldwide automaking. American Motors ran a distant fourth followed by hangers-on like Studebaker-Packard. Detroit's position seemed secure and permanent.

By the mid-1970s a deadly combination of competition from abroad and management myopia had eroded markets until only GM was still profitable. The others were in desperate straits. There was serious talk of a Ford-Chrysler merger; AMC became linked with Renault and companies like Studebaker-Packard disappeared.

German and Japanese automakers saw their opportunity in the smaller car niche. Their exports went up steadily, giving American buyers an alternative to the oversized gas guzzlers from Detroit. The situation was further exacerbated when oil, once

ASKING "JUST RIGHT" BUSINESS QUESTIONS

plentiful and cheap, became scarce and expensive. To compound matters, the Big Three purchased short-term labor peace with long-term escalator clauses tied to the cost-of-living indices. Then inflation spiraled upward, making the U.S. auto industry look as if it was riding with worn shocks on a bumpy road to oblivion. Chrysler went to the edge, rescued at the last minute by federal loan guarantees and a sell-off of a valuable piece of the company. Top management was overhauled when Lee Iacocca arrived as savior.

Ford rediscovered "quality" and redesigned its automobile lines. It was able to do so because its foreign operations—making smaller cars in Europe—were profitable enough to sustain it during a painful restructuring.

GM, in spite of its mammoth market share, found the going hard. Its early attempts at smaller cars at first failed. The initial answer was downsizing: chop the front end, shorten the back end, and call the results a Chevette. Not many people wanted Chevettes nor did they want the alphabet successors, like the ill-fated X-car whose quality problems included engines dying in action and wheels falling off in motion. At last GM looked for help from Japanese technology for design and automation for assembly.

The American automakers switched their labor costs from a high–test mixture to a lower octane. All underwent permanent layoffs of assembly and management people. The Big Three might have saved much time, most of their market, and many of their people, had they asked hard questions before easy answers were adopted.

> *What is really going on in our industry?*
> *What should our planning horizon be?*
> *What kind of managers will we need?*
> *How will we combat foreign competition?*

The experiences of Apple Computer, public broadcasting, and the U.S. automakers demonstrate a truth about questions and

• PROLOGUE •

answers: The answers we are looking for are bound up in the problems we are facing. Those problems are manageable by asking questions that cut to the heart of the issues.

The Ready-Made Answer Syndrome

When faced with rapid change and high levels of complexity, it is tempting to believe that there are simple solutions, sugar-coated and attractively packaged. To exploit that fantasy, books and magazine abound with instant answers to problems. Yet when we attempt to graft onto our organization the solutions that worked somewhere else, the results never match our expectations. The reason is simple: *If someone else's answers are to work for us, we have to duplicate the conditions experienced by them.*

The implied promise of ready-made answers is that if we develop our management styles and organizational designs along the models of successful companies and their leaders, we will experience their successes.

However, before copying them, we should ask how similar were their settings then to ours now: Many of the companies chronicled in books like *In Search of Excellence* were managed for the uneven recession of the 1970s. Once the economic recovery of the 1980s went into full swing, a few of the "excellent" companies changed the approaches responsible for the excellence of the past. They did better than many of the others that stayed with the methods of the '70s—and ran into serious difficulties in the '80s. Before we grab easy answers or try to imitate others, we might ponder these questions:

> *What can we really learn from another organization's past successes?*
>
> *How do we determine what is transferable? What is not?*
>
> *How does the rate of economic change affect attractive solutions from the past?*

ASKING "JUST RIGHT" BUSINESS QUESTIONS

Interdependencies: Indians and Chiefs in the Same Tepee

To find answers by asking questions, those who manage and those who are managed are interdependent. We are, as managers and managees, bound together by the same problems and the same search for answers.

We have a cultural heritage whose emphasis is often on our individuality and on the various role's played by individuals in society. As valuable as that heritage is, it can make efficient team building more difficult. In sharp contrast is the Japanese cultural heritage. In important ways the Japanese heritage is ideally suited to the needs of modern managers and organizations. Because the Japanese value *wa*, or "group harmony," it is easier for Japanese managers to reach collective agreements on managerial decisions. Delegating power comes more naturally since it is never perceived as a threat to anyone's sense of individuality or "territory."

For the needs of modern organizations, group harmony is more compatible than individuality. The Japanese ability to adapt so quickly to the demands of our technological age is partly derived from Japan's cultural heritage. (American-style individuality is more at home with start-ups and the entrepreneurial spirit.)

There is enormous potential for getting answers when the interdependencies between managers are fully exploited. We may have many of the "just right" questions—but unless we elicit answers from those above and below us, the answers may be limited. By raising questions, we can set others to start asking questions, too. The process should be open to the answers we need. Who they are and where they sit is not as important as what they come up with—and whether we as managers are listening to the emerging answers.

Explosive Questions

"Just right" questions are aimed at setting off mental explosions. Unlike everyday conversations, they are carefully crafted

• PROLOGUE •

to move both those askers and answerers to new levels of understanding before taking action.

Asking questions to solve problems is not new. Plato did it in his *Dialogues,* giving Socrates all the good lines. Top management consultants, like Peter Drucker, warn clients that any help is more likely to come as a result of the questions they ask—and not from any answers previously found.

In reading this book, you will be able to use many of the questions "as is." As you get involved in the spirit of the book, the process of "asking just right questions" will be the final payoff.

ASKING "JUST RIGHT" BUSINESS QUESTIONS

THE ANATOMY OF ASKING QUESTIONS

The Phases of a Successful Idea

For us, a successful idea is one that works as planned. When we have a problem, the satisfactory answers are those leading to ideas put to use. If we are short of cash and ask what to do, an answer suggesting we get more cash may not be one we can use. An answer showing us how to change what we are doing to make our cash go farther is one we can use.

Every successful idea passes through three phases. Each phase involves a different perspective. To implement an idea, all three phases need to be eventually integrated. Different thinkers have labeled these phases with various names. We call them *SEEING*, *AIMING*, and *DOING*.

Visualizing What to Do: SEEING

To begin, we need a clear picture of what our challenge is or what our opportunity might be. The process is *conceptualization*. It produces the kinds of questions whose answers flash fresh images of who we are, what we stand for, what our world is like, what it might become. The thinking involves many scenarios, the "what if?" kind of questions.

We can imagine Apple Computer's Steven Jobs and Steve Wozniak conjuring up scenarios in the garage where they started: What would happen if personal computers were available to mass markets? What kinds of computers would make it? How would people use them?

Even when the picture seems clear, we must not allow ourselves to get too comfortable with it. As conditions change, our vision has to be synchronized. Once a concept is solidly frozen, it moves at glacial speed. In the 1960s the American automakers' visions in the boardrooms were headed for the deep freeze while the German and Japanese ideas were cooking away.

Charting the Position: AIMING

In the middle stage of an idea's development we position it. We chart its course toward the place we saw in the *seeing* phase. The *aiming* process calls for a switch to *strategic processes* to get us the blueprint for what we want to do. The result of this long–range thinking is a strategic plan.

In the wake of sharply curtailed federal support, public broadcasting stations began paying a lot more attention to the local demographics and viewing patterns of their particular audiences. What worked for WGBH in Boston was not the answer for KCET in Los Angeles. The answers found by WTTW in Chicago were different from those of WGBH and KCET. Throughout the system, each station had to see itself in scenarios suited to its peculiar market and strengths.

Activating the Plan: DOING

In the third stage we become *operational*. Our concerns are with the practical matter of getting up and getting going; the focus is pulled tightly around the actions needed to reach our objectives.

When General Motors grasped the true nature of the foreign challenges to its automotive dominance, it failed to seek strategic change as a response and opted instead for tactical changes. The problems posed by increased foreign competition did not automatically mean an acceptance of reduced market share. The tactical shifts seemed to work for a while. Ultimately, their failure led GM to concentrate its energies on developing cars differently in response to an evolving market. GM's *seeing* and *aiming* functions were in no better shape than its *doing*. Finally, the total systems overhaul required new managers in new factories — even factories in new places. Past practices were of little help. Asking the right kinds of questions about new realities was the key.

Integrating the Three Stages

The full value of *seeing*, *aiming*, and *doing* comes when they are integrated. Questions like:

What business are we really in?

What are our strategic objectives?

and

What are our tactics?

are part of a broader mosaic. The answer to any question interacts with others. For purposes of discussion and analysis, we separate the questions into conceptual, strategic, and operational—*seeing, aiming*, and *doing* categories. At the end of the process, however, the interrelationships and overlaps lead to integration.

When integrated, the phases—and the next three chapters of this book—look like this Questions Table:

Phase	**SEEING**	**AIMING**	**DOING**
Process	Conceptualizing	Strategizing	Operating
Example Question	What business are we really in?	What are our strategic objectives?	What are our tactics?
Chapter	1	2	3

General Motor's ability to continue integration of the three stages will be the acid test for its ability to remain a dominant automaker. For years its vision was to be the biggest in market share and profitability. Its strategy called for offering cars to every significant market niche. For years, GM's operational thinking was top-down—in other words, what went on in assembly lines was carefully planned from above, light-years before implementation. It was prompted by achieving savings from planning a

· PROLOGUE ·

few basic auto designs and then breaking them out into a variety of models. Thus one Cadillac model could have a Chevrolet engine, and Buick and Oldsmobile parts could be interchangeable. For purposes of marketing, there were many models and even more options to sell. For operating purposes, systems were designed at the top for questionless implementation below.

This top-down approach started to unravel under the pressures of the foreign import threat, inflation, and recession of the 1970s. For the company to aspire to any leadership role, the key was a radical rethinking of operations to continue the strategy and hold to the vision.

The Saturn automobile effort symbolized the challenge: It was a genuine departure in design. Some of the materials from Saturn was new to automobiles. The assembly plant placed human beings and robots in relationships reminiscent of science–fiction scenarios. Comment from assembly–line workers, unheard of in the past at GM, was required. It takes place in Tennessee, not Michigan or California or Ohio. The distribution of the auto is also different from past practices. A "fixed price" policy may anticipate the future.

If this continues to work, then what? Will it be a model for the rest of GM, an integration of *seeing*, *aiming*, and *doing*, which alters each stage as it integrates it with the other two?

ASKING "JUST RIGHT" BUSINESS QUESTIONS
THE QUESTIONING MINDSET

Question Techniques

Any question can be asked in different ways, depending on the intended results. Answers alone, for instance, may not be the only goal. "Just right" questions can affect attitudes and perceptions. They can be asked to start a process.

For the purposes of this book, there are three basic question-asking techniques:

1. *Startling: The surprise question.* The intent is to be creatively upsetting. When a reporter asks a politician an adversarial question, the purpose is to shake truth loose, to cut through obfuscation and evasion. It may be intended to show others whether questions are being answered or evaded.

We can sense when issues are being avoided, intentionally or accidentally. People tend to become comfortable in their habits, even when those patterns are no longer suited to what they are doing. Our intent may be to follow a line of questioning to disrupt the status quo as a first step in getting people to rethink where they are going and how they are getting there.

Illustration: A classic business question is *What business are we in*? Asked in a confrontational style, it could be stated:

> **What makes you think we are still in the business we say we are?**

Questions asked that way are confrontational. The intent is to open eyes and challenge assumptions.

2. *Supporting: The helping question.* An experienced trial lawyer avoids asking questions whose answers he/she is not certain of. In a trial, lawyers use questions to promote their own understanding of the case to the judge and jury. Any discovery of information should happen *before* the trial starts. Questions can be employed to help "discover" what the questioner already knows. When people find out things on their own—or even think

• PROLOGUE •

they are doing so—they are more likely to embrace new knowledge and be more supportive of it.

We may understand perfectly how our business is changing. To get other people on our wavelength, we could ask the questions neutrally: *What business are we in?* There may be no surprise answers for us. Our objective is merely to bring others along. A word of caution, however: As smart as we may be; as clear as our vision is; the answers may spring new ideas on us. Supportive questioning can turn into informative answering.

3. *Searching: The inquisitive question.* A genuinely inquisitive style is best suited to finding out what we don't know but need to know. The purpose is to increase knowledge in the asker and answerer. Everyone benefits because the questions are taking us all to new insights. If we are concerned about the business we are in, the emphasis should be on the spirit of inquiry.

What business are we really in?

The questions in this book are intended to be asked in an inquisitive spirit. The addition of a word or phrase, the tone of delivery, the lifting of an eyebrow, the timing, can convert them to startling or supportive modes. We leave that decision to you with this caveat: Whatever the mode of the question, be sure the way you ask it is intentional. Questions can be interpreted as startling when they were meant as supportive or inquisitive. You should constantly scrutinize your questioning style.

Inner and Outer Voices

The questions in this book are likely to be used in meetings. Therefore, they are going to be spoken with our "outer voices."

We also have "inner voices." We hear them when we are thinking things through, whether by ourselves or in the midst of meetings where others are talking and we are supposedly listening.

The questions in this book can be asked in either the inner or outer voice. You may find the most beneficial applications when they start with our inner voices and then are launched with our outer ones.

No Final Answers

The best questions are open-ended, thereby resulting in useful answers that keep evolving. When we visualize scenarios in the *seeing* phase, we need to know the answers found then may be altered by the questions from the *aiming* and *doing* phases. The *aiming* phase is like being at sea: The port stays in the same place but factors of winds and tides change our charting activities. When we reach the *doing* phase, changes in speed and direction will result from alterations in how we do things on board the ship.

• PROLOGUE •

USING THIS BOOK

"Just Right" Questions: Chapters 1, 2, and 3

The *seeing*, *aiming*, and *doing* chapters are composed of a series of question units. Each unit develops a broad "just right" question such as:

What business are we really in?

and expands its implications through a series of follow-up questions such as:

What business will we be in a few years from now?

and

What businesses could we be in?

The question units are in a logical order, but that order is not rigid. After reading some question units you may find yourself wanting to return to earlier units because of the way you can combine them to meet your special needs.

The "just right" question units are independently useful and collectively powerful. You will be able to use many of the questions just as you find them. More important, when the idea of this book's approach "takes," then you will find yourself asking "just right" questions of your own devising.

Epilogue: The Road to Implementation

All of us have gotten hold of super ideas only to see them unimplemented. It's a familiar scenario: We read a book or article, attend a seminar, or take a course showing us an idea we know would be valuable. Then we return to a reality of hardened resistance. What our reading or studying too often gives us is an idea without the means to make it happen. If this book and its questions have applications for your organization, then the next step is implementation. We see the process of implementing in this manner: First comes understanding and acceptance by your colleagues and organization. Then you must assure there is a commitment to use the idea in a structure that demonstrates its value,

ASKING "JUST RIGHT" BUSINESS QUESTIONS

i.e., a "forward planning" session. To facilitate a question-asking approach for an answer-producing payoff, we provide a series of questions to be thought about and asked.

Additional Reading Suggestions

We have provided an annotated list of books and articles to help you with the process of question formulation. In addition we suggest reading certain magazines, newspapers, and journals to stay on top of what is happening "out there" and what could affect you and your organization.

The Questions List

The following page has a list of the questions that begin each question unit in this book. It gives you a summary of how the next three chapters are organized. When seen together, the interrelatedness will emerge. You will probably see some questions in each category that you will immediately wish to explore.

An Option

Your motivation for having bought this book may be a specific professional problem faced by you or your organization. If that is the case, we suggest you summarize the problem as you now see it. It need not be an elaborate analysis or discussion. In fact it might fit on a three-by-five index card, which can also double as a bookmark.

As you read this book some questions may strike you as appropriate to the problem on the card. If so, you might want to add some notations or rephrase what you wrote.

• PROLOGUE •
THE QUESTIONS LIST

SEEING

What business are we really in?
What is our identity?
Are we innovators or augmentors?
What are our thinking patterns?
What are our resources?
What are our assumptions?

How does the future look?
What risks should we take?
How do we develop our goal?
What are our alternatives?
What about starting over?

AIMING

What is our strategy?
What do we want to happen?
What is the organizing principle?
What is our complexity level?
What segments are we seeking?
What is the attraction?
What are our resource origins?
What are the trends?
How conducive are the conditions?

What special factors influence our business environment?
What consequences are we setting in motion?
Who are our audiences?
What are the readiness levels?
What is the process for objective evaluation?
What is our strategic option?

DOING

What are our tactics?
Where are the bottlenecks?
What kinds of managers do we need?
How do we maintain control?
How do we achieve power integration?
How do we stay in the here–and–now?
What is really going on?
How does our communication of objectives take place?
How will we secure commitment?

How do we handle role expectations?
How do we achieve productivity?
How do we get feedback?
How are we managing our resource base?
How do we accomplish decision implementation?
What is the commonality?
How do we design useful measurements of results?
How effective and efficient is our operation?
What are the change indicators?

ASKING "JUST RIGHT" BUSINESS QUESTIONS

Chapter 1
SEEING

When looking at the same thing, are we *seeing* the same thing?

ASKING "JUST RIGHT" BUSINESS QUESTIONS
WHAT BUSINESS ARE WE REALLY IN?

Reintroducing Ourselves to Our Business

Without a doubt the most famous business and management question is the celebrated *What business are we in?* It is from a famous essay by Harvard Professor Theodore Levitt entitled, "Marketing Myopia." The question was about railroad tycoons of the 1930s who, had they been asked the question, would have answered, "The railroad business." They did not grasp they were really in the transportation business.

Their successors learned it the hard way. Because the railroad tycoons saw their business narrowly, they set the industry on tracks leading American railroads into a dead end in the 1940s and 1950s. Had they seen themselves in the transportation business, the insight might have led to purchases of fledgling airlines like TWA or Pan American. Linking two modes of transportation could have made the rail and airline businesses complementary instead of competitive. The railroaders judged the future by the past, thereby missing the growth opportunities of the transportation business. Instead, automobiles and airlines, trucks and buses changed the way Americans traveled.

Since the reality of *change* has to be factored into our decisions, we have to consider how change can alter the business we have been in: It may no longer be the same or stay the same much longer.

> *What business are we really in?*
>
> *What business will we be in a few years from now?*
>
> *How would our competitors answer these questions?*

In 1978 the airline industry started down the path of deregulation. Companies used to being regulator-responsive, had to become market-responsive. It meant evolve or perish. Competitive forces were unleashed through fare war, route raiding, acquisitions and new ways of looking at operations. The business changed from "transportation" to "transportation services."

Implications of the Question

Questioning the business we are in keeps us loose and limber. Suppose we asked Eastman Kodak: "Are you in the film business or a broader-based business? What conceptual base unites all of Kodak's activities?

Defined too narrowly, the definition could preclude entry into other profitable activities. Example: What would happen if Eastman entered the industrial training market, offering professional education in the uses of its equipment? What if Eastman were to compete with fast film processors like Fotomat by setting up Kodak drop-off kiosks in shopping malls? What would Eastman's prospects be if the emphasis were moved from being a manufacturer of photographic products to becoming a direct retailer of what it already manufactures?

For years Gillette was associated with razor blades. Its theme song advised men to look sharp, be sharp, and use Gillette Safety Blades. Its strategy was to keep the retail price of the razor so low that once purchased, it could sell lots of blades to lots of men. At the time Gillette would probably have defined its business as razors and blades. When it saw the potential in related products such as shaving creams and lotions, the answer would have evolved to shaving materials for men. It was a natural step up to the personal care products business, expanding to a broad range of products for women and men. Its growth may have been in response to a fundamental twist to the question: *What business could we be in?*

Neiman-Marcus started in Dallas as an upscale department store symbolized by its exotic Christmas catalog. At one time, it offered one-of-a-kind products for which there may be but one customer, such as a desk in the shape of a buffalo or his-and-her submarines. Neiman-Marcus eventually decided to expand to other geographical markets where it had to compete with the likes of Saks Fifth Avenue and I. Magnin. What had worked so well for Neiman-Marcus in Dallas did not automatically click in the New York metropolitan area or southern California.

ASKING "JUST RIGHT" BUSINESS QUESTIONS

Were the disappointing sales a result of the company's misunderstanding its business? Might geographical factors have accounted for the success of some Neiman-Marcus stores? (The Dallas store continued to do well during the problems in other locations.) Were the new stores an extension of the Dallas operation or were they in tune with the special needs of the markets where they were located?

What peculiarities are there to the business we are in?

Pondering the Answers

There are no final answers to the question of what kind of business we're in—unless the business winds up in bankruptcy proceedings. When the first satellites were launched, the communications industry saw ways to evolve into telecommunications. Oil was known to be in the ground for a long time before there was an oil refining business. The industry then evolved into the petrochemicals and energy businesses.

The definitions our colleagues have for the business we are in tell us about their perceptions and our communications ability.

If our banker insists we are in the haircutting business when we want to be in the hair-styling business, we may have to go elsewhere for capital or do a better job of educating the banker.

When we ask ourselves and our associates about the nature and definition of our business, consider this question:

What are the implications of fundamentally different answers?

Are visions blurred? Is training needed? Are we making believe we are something other than what we really are? Does it matter?

What is the importance of key players agreeing about the business they are in?

• SEEING •
WHAT IS OUR IDENTITY?

A New Name for New Activities

Had John D. Rockefeller been told that someday the Standard Oil board would approve a new corporate name to match a changed corporate identity, he might have given the prophesier a dime and thought no more about it.

By the time the board settled on Exxon as a new name, the age had passed when anything like a Standard Oil could grow to such mammoth proportions based on oil alone. The oil business had become the energy business. The new Exxon entry into businesses like office equipment and electric motors were attempts to diversify into a future not solely defined in terms of oil-based businesses. To symbolize the change, Exxon said it better than Standard Oil.

Looking for Definition

Who are we?

Are we a high-tech company characterized by young leadership à la Jobs and Wozniak in their heyday at Apple Computer? Are we a service company best known by what our people do? A law firm with antecedents in nineteenth-century Philadelphia? Past comparisons may help:

How do we differ from the way we were?

Later we will be asking much more about objectives. But for now:

What do our objectives tell us about our identity?

If we are subject to scrutiny from without, what others say about us adds to the public perception. What do outside analysts say about us? What kind of press do we have? (Fairly or unfairly, Standard Oil evoked negative images in many people. Exxon allowed the organization an opportunity to remake its image.)

How our customers perceive us can shape our identity, even to the point of altering our view of ourselves. If the change from

Standard Oil to Exxon altered the public's perception the way it was intended how would that be known?

> *What outside evidence will we use to test our definitions of ourselves?*

Organizational Culture

Identity questions lead to asking about our leadership's collective personality. Exxon's leadership took a hard look at the future and tried to position the organization to aim at it. The railroad tycoons of the 1930s fixated on the past. Some analysts believe that the older the average age of the board of directors is, the fewer risks it is willing to take. The *characteristics* of our organization's leadership are bound to influence any visions we have.

> *What characteristics are needed by top management to support what we want to do?*

If they do not share our vision, we may have a problem:

> *What can be done to instill organizational characteristics needed but not present?*

As long as AT&T was a regulated monopoly, its leadership could focus on research and development and take profitable operations for granted. The moment AT&T was plunged into a competitive environment through deregulation and divestiture, its leadership had to be receptive to marketing and more efficient operations.

Organizational *values* are a derivative of organizational characteristics. If our values are at variance with our identity, we need to probe further:

> *What are our organizational values?*

> *What is the consistency between our current values and our future plans?*

An expanded vision can transform identity:

> *What values are needed to do what we plan?*

Change versus Transformation

In the introduction to this book we discussed change as the dominant factor faced by most managers. Asking people and organizations to change personal and corporate values is nearly like asking for a change in genetic structure. Deep-seated values arise from a mix of social cultures, economic realities, personality traits of managers, and other forces that help develop whatever values emerge.

At AT&T the culture had been bred from an organizational structure that for decades had prospered in a protected, regulated environment. The resulting values were consistent with a massive organization as self-sufficient as management could make it. Hiring and retention practices were aimed at keeping employees until retirement. Promotions were from within and layoffs were infrequent. Employment security and secured employees were a given.

When thrust into a competitive world where profit margins could no longer be guaranteed by sympathetic regulatory agencies, AT&T found itself concerned about productivity and competition. It was no longer enough to do a job well; it had to be done well and *productively*—or risk losing business to competitive forces.

Transformation may be evolutionary or demanded in a nanosecond. Our perception of our environment (economic, technological, etc.) is the critical factor.

If our business definition of our environment alters in ways requiring us to redefine our values, how will we handle it?

How should we approach the need to rethink our values?

Because values can be deeply ingrained in us, we may experience resistance to change. We may contend that our values are growing—but our actions may not support the contention:

If we commit to an altered value system, what will be concrete signs of genuine change?

ASKING "JUST RIGHT" BUSINESS QUESTIONS
ARE WE INNOVATORS OR AUGMENTORS?

Innovations versus Augmentations

Perhaps it is more fashionable to be called an innovator than an augmentor, but seldom is one truly an innovator. Most innovations turn out to be augmentations. When Avon Industries recruited thousands of "Avon Ladies" to sell cosmetics door–to–door, Avon was augmenting an idea made famous a generation before by the "Fuller Brush Man."

For promotional purposes we may prefer to call what we are doing "innovative." But for *seeing* purposes, we need to sort out the differences between the innovative and the augmentative. If we are innovative, we are in unexplored territories. We may be sailing into new technologies or new market needs. Whatever is making us want to be innovative requires us to pay attention to situations we have never encountered.

At NASA, going into space meant being thrust into conditions where no one could be certain about how things would work. Being a pioneer is exciting and very much part of the American character. It is also filled with unpredictable dangers. Just as the pioneers could not be sure what was on the other side of a mountain range, astronauts have less than certain assurances everything will perform as planned.

Innovation means discovering a new need or creating a new desire in the markets we serve. The first electric light bulb, the transistor, the first computer were innovative products. Innovations do not happen often.

Augmentation is an improvement of what already exists. It may add value, be an extension, or in some other way build on something already in existence and enjoying some degree of acceptance. Augmentations are often labeled as innovations.

Into the Covered Wagons and Over the Rainbows

If we think we are innovators; we need to pass some tests:

What makes our ideas unique?

• SEEING •

Unique means the only thing like it. If we claim to be unique, what is the basis for our assertion?

What new market have we discovered?

What new desire have we created or found?

When synthetic fibers were invented, a new market developed. The market depended on a desire for a greater selection than manufacturers of clothing thought possible.

If we are convinced we are innovating, then we have to be prepared for the unknowns ahead of us. Without a track record to look back on, we need to consider areas like cash flow, schedules, outside supplier reliability, inside support systems, organization, training, distribution and so forth. It is a whole new ball game in which the rules will get written while we play. What preparations are we making?

How are we preparing for the unknowns ahead?

How about the unknown unknowns?

What planning flexibility are we building in?

How willing are we to stay the course?

The pharmaceutical industry depends on innovative products for the big breakthrough. The search for new cures is enormously expensive, tremendously time consuming and potentially unsuccessful. The successful companies are ready for the long haul financially, organizationally and psychologically. If we are truly innovators, we have to be prepared for more surprises than augmentors.

Augmenting Ain't Easy Either

Just because something has already been invented does not make it easy to imitate. *TV Guide* was one of the most successful ventures in the history of magazine publishing. The idea was simple: Nearly every American home has at least one television set in operation several hours a day. To help people choose what to watch, along came *TV Guide*. It publishes regional editions so every subscriber gets customized listings for his/her locale. *TV Guide* is published weekly and has to compete with daily newspapers with TV listings and Sunday supplements outlining programs for the entire week. Yet *TV Guide's* circulation is consistently among the highest for all magazines.

In 1983, Time Inc. chose to publish and heavily promote an alternative to *TV Guide*. Time Inc. had successfully published *Time, Life, Fortune, Money, Sports Illustrated* and *People*. By adding HBO (Home Box Office) to its corporate empire, Time Inc. was in the cable broadcasting market. When Time Inc. decided to compete with *TV Guide*, HBO was contributing as much to profits as all the magazines combined, thereby suggesting that Time Inc. understood the market segment for its new weekly, *TV Cable Week*. Everything pointed to a successful entry.

TV Cable Week was an instantaneous multi-million-dollar fiasco. The regional editions were too complex to manage. (*TV Guide* does that with relative ease because of its long experience in the process.) The magazine's layout was too complicated for people to use easily. It listed all the available programs but not in an accessible manner. (*TV Guide* is disarmingly simple, so it looks easy to imitate.) When new magazines are launched, they usually take years for a readership to get the magazine into the black. The market rejection and resulting losses of *TV Cable Week* were so unexpected that Time Inc. quickly suspended publication and wrote off enormous losses. Past successes, as Time Inc. discovered, are no guarantee of future victories.

Most of us are augmentors who build on what has been done before. Knowing we are augmenting helps us to focus on the changes we are making:

Why are we augmenting this thing this time?

What would happen if we were strictly imitative?

What will it cost to make the augmentation?

An Augmentation from an Innovation

In 1933 IBM had innovated an accounting machine for the banking industry that could revolutionize how banks handled their accounting. The timing was terrible: Banks were closing because of the Great Depression. Survival, not expansion, was on the

• SEEING •

minds of the banking survivors. IBM was able to make some modifications to the machine and sell it to the New York Public Library. Fifteen more years passed before IBM computers found a market other than in science. Then the Information Age dawned and by making augmentations on the 1933 innovation—Univac—IBM placed itself on the road to world leadership in information management products.

ASKING "JUST RIGHT" BUSINESS QUESTIONS
WHAT ARE OUR RESOURCES?

Reevaluating Resources

In the 1960s Standard Oil could have stated its resources as oil reserves owned by or committed to it, patents, real estate and people. By the time it became Exxon, its major resources were its people and the gigantic cash flow it enjoyed from the day the price of oil shot up like a geyser. Exxon used its cash to enter other promising industries—and as a hedge against the time when the oil-based part of the energy business would be less attractive.

Our resources can be as broad as our imagination and vision allow. Ordinarily resources refer to money, personnel, real estate, patents and other tangibles. The idea of resources can be expanded to include intangibles like time or less obvious resources such as the potential hidden in people because of the way we employ them. In defining resources, we should attempt to expand its meaning and our awareness:

How do we define resources?

What resources might be hidden or transformable?

The Sony Corporation builds audio and video equipment for both the industrial and consumer markets. Sony also manufactures video and audio tapes for those markets. Sony saw what it manufactured for others as a resource for itself. It used the video duplicating equipment to enter the prerecorded videotape business. Sony sells a wide range of video programs to distributors for resale to customers. It has seen its manufacturing capacity as a resource, thereby allowing entrance into related markets.

Getting What We Need When Needed

Depending on the size of our organization and its resources, we have to consider availability. A large corporation may have cash or stock for acquisitions, but there may be many subsidiaries seeking to buy other companies. We must evaluate not only the resources we will need, but their accessibility when we will be needing them.

• SEEING •

What are the guarantees the resources will be available when needed?

The level of support we enjoy one day can change the next. Better opportunities may present themselves to the organization or economic conditions may change.

What would happen if the resources we depend upon were to become unavailable or less available?

Exxon does not control the price of oil—market conditions control the price. If the price slips, Exxon might restrict the resources available for exploring new industries.

We cannot prepare for every imaginable contingency, but we can anticipate some. Example: If we use water to cool equipment, what do we do during a drought? If our capital depends on economic conditions, what will we do in a downturn?

What kinds of reallocations of resources can be made? Substitutions?

Paper Tiger: Ted Turner's Magic Trick

In 1985 Ted Turner, founder of the Turner Broadcasting System, tried to acquire CBS. His plan rested on his ability to leverage existing resources. He planed to issue stock in TBS, establish its value, and offer the shares to CBS stockholders in exchange for their CBS certificates. The plan did not work because CBS and much of the investment community were able to convince CBS's stockholders that Turner had inflated TBS's real worth. The process could have resulted in these questions:

What will activating newly discovered resources cost?

What penalties might there be in using them?

What permanent changes will occur when the resources are used?

Saving the Resources by Changing the Business

Each year the number of Americans involved in agriculture and related industries decreases. Education, chemicals and sophisticated farm equipment have resulted in increased yield-per-acre to the point where, with fewer farmers, there are greater surpluses. Farm land is a different kind of resource. In the richest farming areas, the land can be more valuable when turned into industrial and housing development sites. In other instances small farms are only profitable if they are collected into giant agribusinesses where expensive equipment can be amortized on the basis of mass acreage.

How would our resources look after we answer this question:

> ***What more profitable uses might there be for the resources we control?***

• SEEING •
WHAT ARE OUR ASSUMPTIONS?

Different Assumptions, Different Directions

When World War II ended, the heads of the two retailing giants—Robert Wood at Sears, Roebuck and Sewell Avery at Montgomery Ward—came up with different scenarios based on opposite assumptions about post–war America.

Montgomery Ward's Avery was a traditionalist conditioned by the Great Depression. According to what always was supposed to happen to capitalist economies after major wars, he assumed another depression was inescapable. It had happened before in America and Europe. Therefore, he got ready for it by battening down the hatches, not by planning for growth.

Sears' Wood read the same history books and operated in the same world. What he saw, however, was a massive expansion of industrial capacity about to be transformed from military hardware to consumer products. GM was not going to make tanks, it was going to make cars. Synthetic fibers that replaced natural fibers during the war would open up a wide range of choices in consumer clothing. And so on. He expected an unprecedented boom based on pent-up demand, not another bust.

Sears, Roebuck was steered along a path leading to more stores in more places with more products on their shelves. Record employment levels would make dollars available. Robert Wood became a peacetime hero at Sears.

Montgomery Ward was ready for the depression that never came. By the time the depression assumption was understood to be wrong, Avery was on his way out and Montgomery Ward never recovered.

Digging Up Assumptions

All major assumptions need periodic airing. Most managers are comfortable about stating the assumptions from which they are operating. Normally there are also unstated assumptions derived from past concerns. A successful enterprise may assume—without ever saying so—that past successes assure future successes.

What are our major assumptions?

How current are our assumptions?

When we ask about assumptions, are we hearing conventional wisdom, hand–me–down thinking, or the things we have been saying for years?

What is the history behind our assumptions?

An assumption is not suspect just because it is conventional or traditional. The concern is for current relevancy of assumptions whose original conditions may no longer be operating.

What are the possibilities that our assumptions may be wrong?

Until the oil embargo of 1973 America assumed the permanence of abundant, inexpensive energy. Whether using a 750-watt toaster or driving an automobile using 12 mpg, cheap energy would be there. Just plug it in or fill it up! Since assumptions about energy were never stated, the change from inexpensive to expensive energy was a shock.

What assumptions might we be hiding from ourselves?

Intuitive Thinking

Intuition plays a role in bringing assumptions to the surface. Genuine intuition results from insights percolating up from previous knowledge and experience. Henry Ford supposedly could hold five carburetors in his hands and, without taking any apart, identify a faulty one. By raising a concern about assumptions, we try to raise our consciousness of them. Robert Wood could have read the polls at the end of World War II telling him that experts expected another depression. Economists and history books could have pointed toward that gloomy conclusion as well. We suspect that Wood's intuition played a role in his assumptions about the performance of the post World War II economy.

The Icebergs Will Get You Every Time

Facts and assumptions can be confused with each other. Losing the distinction risks a disconnect with reality. Were facts or assumptions supporting the idea of the unsinkability of the *Titanic*? Perhaps the engineers believed the ship was built so well it could withstand any collision with any iceberg. Or maybe they believed the *Titanic's* route would never bring it close to dangerous icebergs. All the assumptions in the world could not save the *Titanic* when it hit a big iceberg at too much speed and the wrong angle.

Before the near-catastrophe at Three Mile Island, stated assumptions abounded about the reliability of gauges and back-up systems. Those assumptions stood up. The unstated assumptions about the observational capacities of human beings to monitor the systems are where the trouble started. Similarly, when conducting the ill-fated test at Chernobyl, it was assumed by the Russians that everything was under control.

What assumptions could undo us?

Sorting Assumptions from Facts

Facts are scientifically demonstrable. Assumptions are ideas we take for granted, whether factually based or resting on wishful thinking. Intuition mixes fact and assumption. A manager's hands would be tied too tightly if the manager could work only from facts. It is the differences we want to know about.

What are the facts?

What assumptions are we making?

What is the role of intuition?

What do we do about risky assumptions?

What do we do about assumptions in need of change?

ASKING "JUST RIGHT" BUSINESS QUESTIONS
HOW DOES THE FUTURE LOOK?

The Planning Horizon

Are we myopic or farsighted? If farsighted, how far is far? Our distance vision should be determined by practical needs. A member of the House of Representatives is likely to have a shorter horizon than a senator because a representative is elected every two years, a senator every six. If we are in an organization where quarterly reports make or break us, our distance vision is going to be shorter than in another organization seriously involved in a five-year plan. If we are a fledgling organization, our horizon may be tied to how long our cash can last.

What is our planning horizon?

How adequate to our needs is our horizon?

What determines the horizon?

If based on administrative convenience, for instance, our horizon may be more in tune with our organization's needs than with our market's needs. If we claim to be market-driven, our horizon is misplaced.

Example: Educational objectives are tied to the length of a school year, not to the time different people require to learn a subject. The horizon is based on administrative considerations rather than learning realities.

Trend Watching

How do we keep track of trends?

Organizations and managerial professionals have to watch for trends the way the *Titanic's* crew should have watched for icebergs. Trends can present opportunities as well as dangers. Either way, we have to spot them before we can do anything about them.

What are the signs signaling support or nonsupport of our predictions?

• SEEING •

Once, people looked to the heavens for a sign. Now everywhere we look, we have signs of trends: Interest rates, demographics, technological studies, customer preference panels, daily sales reports, newsletters, consultants, think tanks and polls of every sort.

Are we watching the right trends? Are we correctly connecting the trends we are watching? If the price of oil is important to us, is it enough to know the barrel price of crude on the open market? Should we hire a staffer who is fluent in Arabic so we can study middle eastern newspapers?

What trends might connect with each other and influence our future?

Technological breakthroughs and unexpected mergers can alter the future in unsettling ways. Yet there is hardly a technological breakthrough that is a complete surprise to people who closely scrutinize scientific journals. Some mergers catch the business world by surprise, but most do not. The signals usually appear in the financial dailies well ahead of the actual events.

My Crystal Ball or Yours?

Pick a time a few years ago. Think of all the events affecting you and your organization since then. How much of what happened were you able to predict well in advance? Was anything unforeseeable? What was foreseeable but not seen? What turned out differently from what was expected?

What has our track record been in predicting the future?

If your organization has done well over the last few years, was it because of predictive powers or coping powers?

How have we dealt with the unexpected?

A conundrum: The more we know about forecasting techniques, the less comfortable we are about forecasts. Economists make a living doing forecasts, but how many get rich forecasting stocks and bonds? No matter what kind of day it has been on Wall Street, different economists see trend lines differently—but based on the same facts.

ASKING "JUST RIGHT" BUSINESS QUESTIONS

What is our way of looking at the future?

Do we study the past to figure out the future? Do we match current performance against a standard from the past?

> *What parts of the past would be safe guides to the future?*
>
> *What parts of the past are vulnerable to different conditions in the future?*

If forecasts are important to us, we need to know how the forecasts are being made. Forecasting techniques vary from simple projections to very sophisticated manipulations involving several variables. The more complicated the forecasting procedures are, the greater the risk of believing the forecast because of the method. We need to know enough of the forecasting process to be certain it is still connected to the information we think is vital to the future. We need to have answers to these questions:

> *What quantitative models are used in making our forecasts?*
>
> *What is our level of awareness of the numbers being used? The values being assigned to them?*
>
> *What assurance do we have that these models are "fit" for the future?*

Seeing Scenarios

When we hitch imagination and analysis to our forecasts, we may be able to see a number of insightful scenarios. If conditions are subject to change, is the forecast limited by too great an emphasis on the numbers themselves? By *beginning* with the forecast—not ending with it—we can project ideas alongside the numbers to get at important "what ifs." If the automotive forecast is based on sales in a recession, what happens if we enter a boom? If interest rates change significantly, how will sales be affected? How do we quantify what our competitors might be doing?

A scenario allows us to project qualitative and quantitative inputs about what may happen within our planning horizon.

What are possible scenarios regarding our situation in the future?

How can we prepare for the different scenarios?

The Serendipitous

Then there is the unexpected: a wondrous error by the competition, a change in the law, events no one could have foreseen opening "windows of opportunity." John D. Rockefeller never set out to be in the oil business.

At the start of his career, oil was not thought of as an energy source to replace coal. Coal had replaced wood and that was the end of it. In the 1850s Rockefeller clerked, doing his work in the light of lamps lit by whale oil. In 1858 he left to form a commission merchant business called Clark and Rockefeller. Quite coincidentally the business was located in a part of Ohio then awash in oil. At the start Rockefeller's interest was in how to transport oil from the well to the refinery and capture a percentage. Much time passed before he recognized oil as the coming energy source.

It was on his doorstep for years—an accident of geography and history. When he saw how control of sources and refinement were the keys to a fortune, his interest grew.

In what ways can we prepare for the serendipitous?

ASKING "JUST RIGHT" BUSINESS QUESTIONS
WHAT RISKS SHOULD WE TAKE?

Risking More Red Ink

Ballantine Books, a paperback publisher owned by Random House, was losing money so fast its future was in question. Across town at CBS, the Fawcett Books subsidiary was also a loser. To complicate CBS's life, CBS was under pressure from the government to get out of certain businesses. Random House was trying to figure out a way to turn Ballantine around. It hit upon a scheme to buy Fawcett from CBS, merge it into Ballantine, and make two losers into one winner. The risk was that the red ink pool from Ballantine would turn into a sea when joined with Fawcett.

Random House's risk questions could have been these: Are the Fawcett and Ballantine lines competitive or complementary? Are both houses in the red because of unavoidable costs inherent in publishing paperbacks? Are both companies' problems rooted in market rejection? What economies of scale might be found in combining editorial, manufacturing, and warehousing operations? If all the book lines were together, what marketing advantages might there be?

Ballantine turned around faster than a ballet dancer in a pirouette. The combined volume generated by the two companies was supported by a single operation that economically integrated the two previous operations under one roof. Ballantine became a star performer and was able to make additional expansions.

Profiles in Risk

A short psychology lesson: There are people who are drawn to risky situations, inveterate risk-takers who thrive on living on the edge. At the other end of the spectrum are risk-avoiders who will dodge any unfavorable odds to avoid putting their status quo on the line. These extremes should remind us that sometimes risks are sought or ducked for psychological motivations having little to do with organizational needs. If you are being urged to accept

• SEEING •

or avoid certain risks by anyone with a brighter than ordinary gleam in his/her eye, think about this:

What motivates this risk-taker?

What scares this risk-avoider?

Once beyond extraordinary motivations in risk-seeking and risk-avoidance, we should consider the risk ramifications of important actions:

What does "risk" mean to us?

What is involved and what could be lost?

What effects would the loss entail?

Usually, "money" is the first response. "Time" is usually next. Questions need to be asked of other matters, such as organizational distraction, lost opportunities, market position, board confidence and so on.

How comprehensive is our risk analysis?

A formalized approach considering risks is called SWOT Analysis. One of its features is to relate risks to rewards to get at a balanced view of the risks we are investigating.

How might we benefit from a SWOT Analysis?

Strengths ⟷ Weaknesses

Opportunities ⟷ Threats

When Ballantine absorbed Fawcett, it discovered that weaknesses in the two organizations could be converted to strengths by absorption of overlapping positions. The cost-cutting opportunities exceeded the risk of people loss. The existing Ballantine staff could handle the Fawcett books.

Whenever an organization changes, there is the risk of people being distracted by so much new information and activities that their energies will be disproportionately drained. A SWOT risk analysis tries to balance advantages and disadvantages:

What are the opportunities in taking this risk?

What opportunities will we lose?

ASKING "JUST RIGHT" BUSINESS QUESTIONS

What strengths will we have in facing the risk? What weaknesses will surface?

How will our resources be burdened or enhanced?

What has our past risk-coping skills indicated about our future prospects?

Risk Think

We have met executives who believed they were exploring risks by turning the tables with questions like these: "If it were *your* business, what would *you* do? If it were *your* money, how would *you* spend it?" Hypothetical questions are inherently weak. Because it is neither your business nor your money, the psychological burdens cannot be transposed so easily. The approach suggests there has never been enough responsibility delegated, making the exercise into a charade.

Better to examine ourselves as we are:

What kind of risk-takers are we?

Are we riverboat gamblers? Prudent banker types? Cool analytical operators? How objective are we with other people's money? Our own? How well would we handle success? What does failure do to us?

What would be the consequences of failure?

How prepared for failure is our organization?

How prepared for success are we?

What would be the consequences of success?

There is also the matter of staying the course, hanging in there. Our ability to do that depends on the interplay between our psychological staying powers and the organizational support and conviction behind us. If we are planning a new venture or project, there is a natural tendency to be optimistic and supportive at the start. It is an opportune moment to build in some buffers to prepare for any trying times ahead.

What preparations are there for staying the course?

• SEEING •

In the beginning, expectations can be raised as high as our enthusiasm can take them. It is the Garden of Eden scenario: a choice piece of real estate, wonderful climate, good neighbors, plenty of food. What could possibly go wrong? Let's call it "Paradise" and not hold back in the expectations department. Why, even the snakes will love it!

What kinds of expectations are we creating as we overcome cautions about risk?

ASKING "JUST RIGHT" BUSINESS QUESTIONS
HOW DO WE DEVELOP OUR GOAL?

Set the Goal, Then Write the Objectives

We define a *goal* as the place to be reached at the end of the race. To measure progress in getting there and to further define the goal, we establish *objectives* or points along the way. (In some organizations the two are reversed: Objective is the end, and goals the points along the path.) In this book a goal is broader than an objective.

If we "manage by objectives" (commonly called MBO), the sensible approach is to agree on the goal between the manager and the managee. Then continue with development of specific objectives. If we are building a strategic plan, our goal may be broadly stated. The objectives will be more tightly drawn. Together, the goal and objectives require clarity to become a standard by which our activities will be judged.

In new ventures, a reciprocating relationship develops between a goal statement and its accompanying objectives: The goal may sound extremely good until the more defined objectives cause a restatement of the goal. That phenomenon does not mean the goal is faulty. Instead it shows a form of growth of our understanding of what we are about or of changes we had not anticipated in our market or organization. (In the *Aiming* chapter we will deal with strategic objectives. For now we concentrate on the goal.)

A Sweet Goal

In making the historical decision to sweeten its formula, Coca-Cola's goal could have been stated like this: *Coca-Cola is to remain the dominant soft drink in the world.* Top management at Coca-Cola saw shifts in taste preferences as a long-term threat to Coke's top position. Consumers in the younger age brackets preferred sweeter drinks like Pepsi-Cola. The trend pointed to a historical shift. In the past people in younger age brackets preferred Coca-Cola to Pepsi-Cola and other sweeter drinks in large enough numbers to assure Coca-Cola's lead in later years.

Any preference shifting in habit-forming years therefore sets off alarms in the places where those numbers are tracked. Because shifts to sweeter drinks had been unprecedented in the past, even a small shift pointed toward a large loss of market share in the years ahead. (It is worth noting Coca-Cola's planning horizon had long-distance vision.)

The background in formulating a goal provides information about it:

How have our goals been developed?

What is the history of a recent goal?

For Coca-Cola the background was in monitoring trend changes of various population groups, holding taste tests, examining how choices made by individual trend setters affect the choices of their acquaintances, and performing other market studies. The decision to change the formula was based on solid market evidence of a growing change in soft drink consumption preferences.

Goal Alignment

An acid test for a goal in its formative period is to see how well it stacks up to what went on in the *seeing* process. What we are looking for is not perfect harmony—in a growth situation ideas may still be fluid—but for the goal to be an extension of our basic concepts:

How does our goal connect to the business we are in?

If we are Exxon, how does the entry into electric motors fit with the main business?

How does our goal fit our identity?

At Sears, Roebuck, the post-World War II goal of rapid expansion meant redefining the Sears of the past. Later, Sears' decision to go into a full range of financial services was consistent with its identity as an organization sensitive to how spending patterns are changing.

What does the goal suggest about decisions to innovate or augment?

ASKING "JUST RIGHT" BUSINESS QUESTIONS

What demands will our goal make upon our resources?

For Coca-Cola, the sweeter formula decision sent reverberations throughout the massive organization: Marketing had a whole new game to play. Manufacturing and distribution had to change to accommodate the new Coca-Cola. New products had to take a back seat to the introduction of New Coke.

What assumptions are bound up in our goal?

Coca-Cola's initial assumptions were clear: The shifts in taste preferences were fundamental and permanent. Replacing the old Coca-Cola with the new Coca-Cola would be accepted by Coca-Cola drinkers and tried by others. On the basis of taste test preferences and extrapolations about the future, Coca-Cola saw a "Pepsi Generation" threatening Coca-Cola's historical dominance.

What risks are involved in the goal?

Coca-Cola knew some people would regret the passing of the old Coca-Cola, that there might be some diehards who found a substitute for the old Coke hard to swallow. Management reasoned, however, that the risks would be offset by the rewards of holding on to the dominant market position.

Goal Clarity

In later stages, the goal will take on additional clarity through the process of setting objectives. In the *seeing* stage its clarity is developed through the communication process, provided the people who have to support it are within our communication network. The communication system we use is as important to the goal's clarity as is its language.

What communication system is best suited to our goal?

When AT&T started metamorphosing from a protected species into a competitive one, were goals aimed at making those changes best communicated in top-down memoranda? When Coca-Cola attempted the formula switch, how did they lay the communications groundwork with their retail distribution channels?

In transmitting our goal, how have we brought others into the communication loop? Do they see it the way we do? Have they had input?

How clear is our goal to others?

Nods of the head signal agreement—or the onset of a nap:

What evidence assures us that our goals are clear to the key people?

ASKING "JUST RIGHT" BUSINESS QUESTIONS
WHAT ARE OUR THINKING PATTERNS?

Underneath the Analogies

Analogies help others see the pictures in our heads: Walking into the bedroom of a teenager might prompt, "This place looks like World War III." In business comparisons are used to show how much an idea is like a successful idea someone else once had: "This is just like the old 'give them the razor and sell them the razor blades' idea."

Analogies also signal the experiences of the users. By listening carefully to the analogies of others, we can know something of how well they are catching on to a new vision.

What kinds of analogies are being used?

When book publishing companies saw microcomputer software and videocassettes as natural extensions of the publishing business, they were on the right track. But the economics of book publishing are not analogous to the worlds of microcomputer software and videocassettes. Books are manufactured in very large runs to keep unit costs low, a consequence of printing technologies. Videocassettes and software disks can be reproduced "on demand," a result of magnetic tape technology. There is no economic reason to create large quantities of tapes and disks before there is actual demand for them. In determining how to profitably integrate disks and videocassettes within the publishing business, an analogy stating "Videocassettes and software are just like books" is dangerous.

Montgomery Ward's failure to grow after World War II might have been expressed by Sewell Avery in analogies like "this postwar period will be like all the others."

What are the concepts underlying our analogies?

In the days when AT&T was living safely in the "land of regulation", managers were recruited with engineering backgrounds. It made sense: The opportunities for AT&T were in research and new product implementation. Selling products was not the problem, discovering and installing them was. Many of the old hands at AT&T had to grapple with being thrust into the "land of competition". They had to learn to think in market-driven ways, not product driven ways. What are the analogies that would signal when AT&T people had made the leap from regulation to competition?

> *What does an analogy tell us about conceptual deficiencies?*

Corp Think

Intentionally or not, all organizations condition their members to see the world through a particular prism. If we work in the information industry for a company like IBM, information products are more likely to catch our eye than if we work in the agricultural implements business at Caterpillar Tractor. The images likely to attract our attention, the nomenclature we use, and our patterns of thinking are molded by our organization's business. A certain mindset emerges. We need to know our own as well as those of others:

> *What is our dominant mindset?*

> *How well suited is it to the tasks lying ahead of us?*

Where do we draw our comparisons from? Do we see analogies others have not grasped? Do they use analogies we are trying to understand and apply? If we were once amateur athletes, do we use sports analogies in business settings?

> *How can we adjust our thinking patterns to present realities?*

Changing Careers and Positions

Younger professionals are likely to make many career changes. The more successful a person is within an organization, the greater the chance for promotion to different responsibilities and tasks. Whether moving from one industry to another—or up the ladder—the mindset from a previous role is brought along. How will that mindset apply in new settings or with new assignments?

ASKING "JUST RIGHT" BUSINESS QUESTIONS

What is still of use in our thinking patterns?

What—if anything—needs changing?

Most major league baseball managers are former players. How does a former player make the transition from playing to managing? Several years of playing are valuable at the start, but what does he need to learn? If a teacher becomes an administrator, his/her lecturing skills may have worked with students, but how effective will they be with a staff?

What do we need to learn? What do we need to unlearn?

Changing Outlooks and Mindsets

It takes years to impart an adequate education to a human being. As willing to learn as someone might be, it requires time. Conceptual plateaus have to be reached before new heights can be scaled. If we are asking people to take on additional responsibilities or if we are entering new areas as an organization, we must be aware of thinking patterns in need of change. To change anyone's thinking is a slow process, so we need to assess what to do about it and who the candidates are:

Whose outlooks need revamping?

What paths are open for changing outlooks?

An inexperienced manager might be tempted to replace people rather than change them. Usually it is not that easy, nor is it smart. The experience base of the people we have can be their springboard to growth.

A clever and resourceful manager can get changes in thinking by instituting changes in conditions. If we want someone to learn new skills, we might arrange for that person to work with someone whose example and experiences will rub off. Many a fresh second lieutenant has learned how to command from a seasoned sergeant.

If we alter the objectives of a position or in some manner force the position to be handled differently, an old hand in the position may respond better than a recruit. It depends on attitude:

How receptive to change are the people we need to change?

The implication of this unit is that we will be dealing only with subordinates who have to pay attention to what we ask or say. Much of the foregoing applies to our colleagues and superiors as well. We can erase hierarchical lines between us and our subordinates to reach a genuine spirit of inquiry, but whether those above us are willing to see the demarcation lines disappear could be another matter.

How do we involve those above us in our concerns about their mindsets?

How critical are changes in top management's viewpoints?

How might the marketing people at Time Inc. have gotten top management to see that *TV Cable Week* needed to be a *regional* publication? Was the problem a mass circulation mindset used to less regionally sensitive publications like *Life* and *Sports Illustrated*?

What are the consequences of resistance to new ways of thinking from any quarter?

Mercedes-Benz has resisted mass-production techniques that override quality control concerns. By limiting production, it has been able to keep demand high and compensate for selling fewer cars by selling them at very high prices. Will Mercedes-Benz be able to change this thinking pattern if conditions change?

ASKING "JUST RIGHT" BUSINESS QUESTIONS
WHAT ARE OUR ALTERNATIVES?

Selling Technology Instead of Equipment

In 1980 *Fortune* magazine selected Baker International (now Baker-Hughes) as one of the better companies of the 1970s. Baker manufactured oil exploration equipment. In the '70s demand was feverish for new wells and equipment to drill deeper in old wells. Baker expanded its capacity to produce equipment. Expansion caused management to ask questions about additional market opportunities.

One of the divisions saw selling its technology as an alternative to selling products based on that technology. The reasoning was that underdeveloped countries could only afford the technology and would use their own labor to build the products. Baker went to China a few years before the U.S. government recognized the mainland regime as China's legitimate government. The Chinese welcomed Baker's advances and an important deal was struck. Baker's success in China led the company to a profitable program of selling oil exploration technology worldwide. Seeking alternatives broadened an already profitable business.

Baker's decision to explore alternatives did not come at a time of duress. It came when management could have contented itself with tending to the business just as it was because it was doing so well. Consideration of alternatives should not be reserved for when things are coming apart.

Avoiding the Yellow Brick Road

When the achievement of a goal depends upon a series of supporting steps being completed first, we need to ask questions about *contingencies*. If we are shooting a film on location, what is the contingency plan for days when the weather is uncooperative?

> *What situations lie ahead of us where we might need contingency plans?*

We would be more lucky than smart if we knew in advance those points along the way where contingencies were needed. Instead of trying to predict every one, we should think about our readiness to respond to a need for alternatives.

What are our organizational response mechanisms?

Few organizations can afford the counterpart of a fire department—a group of people trained to deal exclusively with emergencies.

Who would we assemble to come up with a contingency plan in an emergency?

Perhaps we do not need alternatives as much as a group that determines what our alternatives will be if the need arises.

The flexibility of an organization to implement alternatives is as important as the alternatives. We should look for procedural blocks that might stall the installation of contingency plans.

What obstacles might be placed in the path of alternatives?

What would ease implementation?

Alternatives and Anxiety

Alternatives can be a threat and a source of anxiety because they imply dissatisfaction. But if they are a normal way of planning for those times when what was supposed to work is not working, their presence will not unduly alarm anyone. There are three golden rules about alternatives:

Thou shalt plan alternatives.

Thou shalt not keep alternatives a secret.

Thou shalt review alternatives.

Baker International reviewed alternatives as a regular part of its self-evaluation. For organizations like Baker, the only thing worse than having alternatives would be having none.

How regularly do we review alternatives?

How open is the process?

Alternatives and Action

Putting alternatives into action should be a deliberative act. Even when they have been planned and the organization has been ready for them, they represent change. We need to ask questions about realism, fallout, and the effects of doing nothing.

Some time may have passed since we designed our alternatives. Therefore we should begin by asking:

> *How realistic are our alternatives in today's world and for the future?*

Are we instituting an alternative as a reflex action, a fad, or because it truly fits a current situation? Are we reacting first and thinking later?

By using an alternative, we are going to create reactions inside and outside the organization. What will they be like?

> *What internal or external fallout patterns might we expect?*

When Baker started selling technology, did it risk a domestic reaction whereby U.S. customers would prefer buying technology too? If so, what would that have done to all the products it sold? When CBS fell from first to third in the rating's race, it laid off people from the News Division as part of its contingency plan. In doing so, might it cause others who kept their jobs to start looking before another ax fell?

We can always find reasons to do nothing. We can "tough out" a sales dip, stick to our knitting, and keep on doing whatever we have been doing just as we have always done it. Doing nothing different can work. But if we choose that path, we have made a choice and need to know its consequences as well:

> *What happens if we do nothing?*
>
> *When should doing nothing different be an alternative?*

• SEEING •
WHAT ABOUT STARTING OVER?

Whither Goes the Bandwagon?

We are now at the end of the *seeing* process. An idea of what we want to do should be emerging. If that idea has resulted from the back-and-forth, give-and-take process of asking "just right" questions, we are almost ready to move to the *aiming* stage.

Before we do that, however, we should pause and reflect: What influence has group think played in arriving where we now are? Group think is a phenomenon discouraging deviations by individuals from what the group wants. It is the pressure to squelch nay-sayers no matter how well-founded their objections.

History is filled with episodes where an action planning group first insulated itself from reality and then convinced itself it was right by closing off channels for objections. The Bay of Pigs invasion and the Watergate break-in are two classic illustrations. President John F. Kennedy assembled a group of planners who hatched a scheme to invade Cuba and overthrow Castro. They gathered faulty intelligence about Cuban military capabilities and dreamed up wishful assumptions about the Cuban people rising up in support of an invasion. The planners made belief in the scheme the litmus test for being part of the group. The invasion was a bloody fiasco that strengthened Castro and weakened Kennedy.

The Watergate break-in was supposed to insure President Richard Nixon's reelection, not lead to his resignation after his reelection. The group, some of them lawyers, suspended reason by agreeing to break the law. They were motivated by missionary zeal about the safety of the republic, but they were also willing victims of believing their own baloney: If one did not support the scheme, he was disloyal to the group and the country—in that order.

Both the Bay of Pigs and Watergate are examples of group think run amok. Both were held together by *consensus*. At its best, consensus connotes a group discussing an issue until it

ASKING "JUST RIGHT" BUSINESS QUESTIONS

reaches a rational decision all members can live with. It is an excellent way to come up with a workable idea, but we need to beware of horse trading and compromises made purely from group dynamics. Has the urge been to get everyone on the bandwagon, or has the urge been to get the bandwagon rolling because we know where we are headed?

> *How did our idea get to its present place?*
> *What was the role of group think?*
> *How did we arrive at consensus?*

If it is a group decision, reasonably done and if there seems to be broad-based support, how would individuals from the group answer this question:

> *What degree of support do you personally and professionally give this idea?*

How willing would individual members be to accept full accountability for the idea? Was each member herded onto the bandwagon or did each climb aboard willingly and enthusiastically? Did anyone want to leave the bandwagon after having boarded it?

Decision-Maker's Remorse

Real estate agents brace themselves for "buyer's remorse." It is the after-signing jitters from having agreed to a major commitment: Did I pay too much? Can I afford it? What did I miss? Any major change in activity patterns can bring on last-minute second thoughts. It can occur at the end of the *seeing* process: Is this idea any good? What have we missed? Should we be doing this? How did we get here?

The normal psychological misgivings have to be sorted out from any legitimately based reasons for recycling the process or any part of it before moving to the *aiming* stage:

> *What advantages could there be to starting over? Disadvantages?*
> *What parts of the seeing stage are worth another look?*

Starting over is not always desirable, but it is an option worth consideration. If it opens up some questions about moving ahead, something important may be going on:

What would happen if we started the whole process over? Some part of it?

Would our credibility be lost? Would credibility be gained? Might the idea be strengthened?

One More Time

Now and then the best advice an editor can give an author is to put the manuscript in a drawer and start over. It is less painful than it sounds: If the author has a vision, trying to salvage it from a faulty manuscript is not as likely to succeed as beginning again. It is not exactly starting over; it can be starting fresh.

We call it the "Kissinger stratagem." Former Secretary of State, Henry Kissinger, was once breaking in a new aide with an important assignment. The aide worked long and hard, did much research, agonized over his analysis, and slaved over every word in his final report. The day came when it was ready and was presented to Kissinger. Without reading a word, Kissinger took the report, looked the aide straight in the eye, and asked, "Is this the best you can do?" The aide, flustered, acknowledged that it might not be his best work. Kissinger handed him the unread document with this dictum: "Do not give me anything until it is the best you can do."

Are we at that place in our thinking where the idea is the best we can come up with? If it is, on to *aiming*! If it is not,

What still needs to be done before we move to aiming?

Chapter 2

AIMING

At his first strategy session the new director threw a dart at the wall. Then he ran to the wall, drew a circle around the dart, and exclaimed, "Bulls-Eye!"

As he grew older, he became wiser: He learned to draw the circle first and throw the dart later.

ASKING "JUST RIGHT" BUSINESS QUESTIONS

WHAT IS OUR STRATEGY?

Strategies of a Lion and a Lamb

An organization's strategy is its grand plan for achieving its goal. It flows best from the answers to questions about the business it is really in. Consider the strategizing by two companies: IBM at the time of its greatest success and People Express, a start-up airline that enjoyed initial success and then went into a nose-dive culminating in its absorption into Continental Airlines.

IBM's goal had been to dominate the information management markets, even as those markets evolved. Frequently it set the trends for its industry. The strategy worked so long as the market demanded mainframe computers for industry. When it failed to see the potential competition from personal computers and networking within the business environment, it became vulnerable to smaller, more adaptable companies.

But in its prime, IBM had the wherewithal to swallow large companies whose skills, products, or markets it sought. It was able to compete with the industrial giants sponsored by the governments of other nations such as Japan. The equipment IBM built to handle the information needs of whole industries defined the information frontiers of those industries. When it saw a new market, it geared up to enter it and alter that market by its entry. IBM's strategy was dominance of any market it entered. All of its activities in a market were in tune with the corporate strategic plan.

When People Express first got started, its strategy was to develop a market for discount flying. Its reasoning was that there were many people who did not fly because they felt they could not afford to. They either did not travel or traveled by cheaper means, such as buses. People's strategy was to find every conceivable way to reduce costs and offer dramatically lower air fares that would attract the attention of infrequent flyers and bargain hunters. It was no accident that People came into existence at the beginning of the new era in airline deregulation. This allowed People Express to compete with the traditional carriers on price and route selection.

The strategies of IBM and People Express were directly connected to and supportive of their organizational goals and their concepts of the businesses they were in at the time. As we will see later, People Express's strategy worked long enough to make it the fifth largest carrier in the USA by 1986. However, the same strategy eventually overtaxed its resources and aroused its competitors. In the 1990s, Southwest Air has followed a similar plan.

> *What is our strategic plan?*
>
> *What is its connection to our goal?*
>
> *How does it flow from the business we say we are in?*

Strategy Articulation

If we asked different people in our organization to define our strategy, what would they say?

> *How clear is our strategy within our organization?*

Would people do their jobs any differently if they saw our strategy the way we do?

> *How do we communicate our strategy within our organization?*

To put their business strategies in place, IBM and People executives began by communicating their vision to their own staffs from top to bottom. The idea was that for business strategies to succeed, everyone in the organizations needed to understand and embrace the plan. Not only was that approach aimed at building loyalty, it enhanced implementation by getting full participation in it. The idea at IBM and People Express was for everyone within the organization to feel—and behave—like a stakeholder or someone who personally and professionally identified with the interest of the organization.

> *How well do our own people know and support our strategy?*
>
> *Are our people spectators or participants in its formulation?*

Structure and Strategy

People Express deliberately set out to build an organizational structure consistent with its strategy. It wanted fewer managerial layers. It needed employees who could play multiple roles in everyday operations. It searched for gates at less expensive airport sites. Everything it did in pursuit of a lower fare structure was aimed at questioning why costs had to be what they were at the traditional carriers and how they might be reduced at People Express.

IBM had three articles of faith: top quality products, the best service program possible, and respect for employees. The organization was built around these tenets. It was willing to invest heavily in product research and acquisition. The organization's internal structure took second place to its external service programs—the customer came before the organization. Its employees were intensely loyal to "Big Blue." The three articles of faith were long ago enunciated by Thomas Watson, Sr., and were instilled in every employee.

Big Blue's strategy could be seen clearly in its development and marketing plans. People Express's strategy explained the differences—good and bad—between its ground and flight personnel and those from the traditional carriers. In its heyday, a flight on People was a trip to another land: There was more of a team spirit by People employees than would ordinarily be found at an older line such as United or American.

How is our organizational structure supportive of our strategy?

How is it disruptive?

If our structure is a carryover from the past, what will changes in strategy mean to it? Example: The communications revolution is changing the ways in which we communicate with each other and our markets and clients. As those information technologies change, opportunities will probably enable us to communicate—and organize—differently.

• AIMING •

How has our structure caught up with our strategy?

IBM's fall from the top shook the organization to its foundations. The strategy that had worked so well for so long lulled management into a sense of invulnerability. IBM management was not ready for the swift change in the markets for mainframes. The irony is worth noting: IBM's strength led to its weakness. The strategy was brilliant for its time. When the time changed, no one at the top of IBM was ready to overhaul it. The market overhauled IBM.

Comparing Our Strategy to Our Competitor's Strategies

When we compare our strategy to those of our competitors, what do we find? Are we missing something or are they? Are there such differences between us that we should expect altogether different strategies? If new opportunities are causing us to change our strategy, is the same phenomenon occurring at our competitors?

What distinguishes our strategic thinking from our competitors?

What in our strategy gives us a competitive edge?

IBM failed to change a winning strategy when it no longer was relevant. Perhaps IBM needed to look more closely at the strategies of its competitors. For a while People Express's strategy attracted enough bargain hunters to sustain its rapid growth. But eventually its strategy overreached itself: It built capacity beyond the market's needs. It became so large so fast that it had to adopt the very tactics of its competition: first class seating, frequent flyer inducements, and all the other frills that drove up costs while trying to attract all segments of the flying market needed to fill unused capacity.

ASKING "JUST RIGHT" BUSINESS QUESTIONS
WHAT DO WE WANT TO HAPPEN?

And Now a Brief Word from the Top

Defining what we want to happen as a result of our strategy is an attempt to put in plain English the results we seek. Many organizations put it into a *mission statement* intended to be an "umbrella" under which are gathered identity, strategy and structure. It is a rigorous exercise always in need of updating and reviewing.

A few years ago American Metal Bearing Company had a stab at refining its mission statement. AMB is a specialized manufacturer of metal bearings and seals. Its mission statement had been:

> *Our mission is to design, manufacture, and market babbitted (i.e., alloyed metal) line-shaft bearings and seals. Our market niche is military shipbuilders within the shipbuilding industry.*

The specificity about what it did and what its market was did not occur after a single attempt. It was distilled from a careful analysis of what AMB had been doing in the past and thought it could be doing in the future.

What would our mission statement say? Could we articulate our plan with our market?

What is our mission statement?

We look for mission statements dominated by verbs and nouns. When there are too many adjectives and adverbs, there are too many "qualifiers." We want a compressed description of what is to happen within our organization and in our intended markets. In the early days, People Express's mission statement might have been:

> *Our mission is to offer lower air fares in densely populated regions. Our niche will be people who seldom fly and frequent fliers in search of bargains.*

Our version of People's mission statement and the actual one from American Metal Bearing describe what is planned at a particular time. The words reflect reality as seen then—and the words need to change when reality alters our actions.

When People Express acquired Frontier Airlines, the idea was consistent only with its strategy of offering as many routes and connections as it could to blanket the country. But because Frontier was an airline whose reputation was built on extra services, its acquisition was one reason for People's reverses: Frontier was not a discount carrier, it had extensive labor contracts (People had none), and its mission statement would have been inconsistent with People's. In addition it was already seriously in the red. People Express was unable to absorb Frontier successfully and, instead, found Frontier to be a drag on its structure, approach and bottom line. People's problems began with the excess capacity represented by Frontier. Eventually it had to sell off Frontier to buy enough time to try to rescue itself. Had People Express seen the contradictions between its mission statement and Frontier's, it might have sought a different acquisition.

For eighteen years the American Metal Bearing mission statement was sufficient. Then a combination of lower-priced products from abroad and shrinking demand from the military altered the picture for AMB: What it had always wanted to happen could no longer happen. With its expertise and resources in the shipbuilding industry, AMB started looking for new products its traditional markets wanted and which AMB could produce. It applied a SWOT Analysis (see page **41** for a discussion of SWOT) and discovered it could develop a proprietary product of its own as well as expand the applications of components it was already making. Its mission statement was revised:

> *Our mission is to design, manufacture, and market a variety of finished products and extended applications of components to shipbuilders.*

The Concrete Content in Objectives

A mission statement like AMB's can aid in the development of useful objectives. Much has been written about writing objectives, managing by objectives, and so on. Cutting through it all, there are two practical guidelines for objectives:

First, objectives must be *measurable*. No matter what the yardstick is, it should refer to something concrete to determine how much of the objective has been met or missed. AMB's objectives could help it measure its success in designing, manufacturing and marketing its products. Additionally it could have developed objectives about market penetration.

Second, objectives must be *achievable*. People Express reasoned that if the price was attractive enough, people who had never flown would fly. At first People met its objectives with full flights. But as the airline expanded its capacity, it failed to meet its objectives. The failure was critical because People Express needed fuller flights than its competition to compensate for the lower profitability levels of its fare structure.

> *What elements in our objectives can we measure?*

> *What is the basis for believing our objectives are achievable?*

Objectives give everyone another way of looking at our major activities. When AMB changed its mission statement, its management could have asked:

> *How consistent is what we say we will do with what we really will do?*

Changing objectives does not, by itself, change actions. Comparing the actions and the objectives is what can lead to changes.

When AT&T moved from a regulated, protected environment to a deregulated, competitive environment, its marketing objectives had to change. Since most of the people charged with achieving the new objectives were holdovers from the past, it was possible for activities to remain the same even though the *aims* had changed. Gauging activities by our objectives helps to show the degree of support for them.

Expectation Construction

Putting the spotlight on new objectives can create expectations beyond our abilities to deliver. Making promises we cannot keep or creating expectations out of line with reality can lead to painful reviews of what we promised, not what we delivered. Start-up situations are particularly prone to this phenomenon. Example: Direct mail campaigns are very successful if the response rate is 2.5 to 3 percent. If we get carried away and suggest we can get a 5 percent rate, then an actual of 4 percent may be disappointing.

What expectations have our objectives created?

How realistic are they?

What is our ability to deliver?

ASKING "JUST RIGHT" BUSINESS QUESTIONS
WHAT IS OUR ORGANIZING PRINCIPLE?

Push the Button, See the Picture

If we were asked to write the mission statement for the Polaroid Corporation, it would say:

> *Design, build, and market photographic products giving instant gratification to amateur photographers.*

The key phrase is *instant gratification.* All of Polaroid's efforts, whether seen internally or externally, are organized around the idea that there is a vast market for photographers who get their pleasure from the finished photograph, not the process leading to it. (The more "serious" photographer would consider instant photos as the work of amateurs.) To get the picture immediately after being snapped, amateurs may have to pay more, sacrifice elements of quality, and be able to use only special cameras and film, but the joy of photography for them is having it now, not later.

Instant gratification is the organizing principle of Polaroid's engineering, manufacturing and marketing efforts. Polaroid upgrades cameras and films to expand its market. Its promotional activities stress the speed with which a user can have pictures.

Pass the Ontological Glue

As we examine strategies and mission statements, we look for the common element hitching everything together: IBM's three tenets of faith—outstanding service, excellent product performance, and respect for individuals—was once the mark of everything IBM did. It put actions behind its words with an extensive service organization, developed superior products, and it trained employees in all aspects of the IBM definition of *superiority.* It was a perfect execution of an organizing principle—but it depended on the high prices IBM could charge for mainframes when the competition was weak.

People Express's organizing principle was *minimal cost*. Its workers were trained to do several jobs and its passenger amenities were pared down to bare bones.

For most of this century, Sears has been organized around *convenience* for the middle class purchaser. When customers were far from stores, Sears mailed them catalogs. When suburbia grew, Sears placed stores in choice locations at malls. When the middle class paid more attention to finances, Sears tried providing additional financial services.

What is our organizing principle?

What common thread runs through who we are and what we do?

What do we offer that our competitors do not?

When we look at any of our major activity categories—research and design, manufacturing, marketing, customer service, etc.—can we find the consistency of our concept? What would our customers, reviewers, regulators, and competitors say is our organizing principle?

What Language Can Tell Us

When an idea resists a simple definition of its organizing principle, it is a signal. If we cannot articulate what we think is our vision, either the idea is flawed or our comprehension of it is incomplete. These questions may keep the juices flowing:

What word or phrase captures the essence of what we are planning to do?

How consistently does that word or phrase fit the different categories of activity?

At Baker International, expansion was the organizing principle leading to the breakthrough to sell technology and products. At Exxon, diversification summed up the drive to find new market areas.

When we have the word or phrase that captures the organizing principle, how do we use it?

ASKING "JUST RIGHT" BUSINESS QUESTIONS

How well understood is the organizing principle within our organization? By our markets?

What is the value of spreading the word?

At IBM and People Express, the companies made their organizing principles known to employees before they started doing their jobs. Technical superiority at IBM and low prices at People became the basis for how employees were to approach their jobs and their customers.

· AIMING ·

WHAT IS OUR COMPLEXITY LEVEL?

The MEGO Scale

In most on-a-scale-of-one-to-ten ratings, we want to be tens, not ones. Not so the MEGO Scale: It is the acronym for "my eyes glaze over," an undesirable reaction when we are presenting our strategy and objectives to any group inside or outside our organization.

The onset of a high MEGO rating is signaled by the heavy eyelid or the restless hands. When we see telltale signs of tune-out, we wonder: "What is our MEGO rating?" When we know a subject better than those to whom we are presenting it, we have to guard against making our material inaccessible. When our material is both *complicated* and *complex*, the MEGO score soars.

Something can be complicated but understood if presented correctly. A printed circuit board is complicated. It is made easier to comprehend when different colors are used to help identify various circuits. The complication is not removed, it is made simpler to track. A strategic plan can be made easier to understand by isolating its organizing principle and mission statement, and then referring to them as the plan is discussed.

Something can be made complex by the presence of many independent variables. In predicting how a market will react, few variables are under our control. In attempting to explain all the possibilities and how they interact with each other, we can introduce a complexity level others might have trouble following. We cannot make complexities disappear. How we present complexity is a key to reducing a high MEGO score.

What is complicated about our plan?

What complexities are in our plan?

What are we doing for the audience to overcome complexities and complications?

Avoiding Tune-Out

We know an author-psychologist who subjects his manuscripts to a rigorous readership test. He selects a group of people similar to the intended readership. Each person is asked to read the manuscript and mark wherever his/her reading was interrupted for any reason. If the reader needs a cup of coffee, remembers something that has to be done right away, or simply stops, the author wants to know where the interruption occurs. When all the test copies are back, the author compares stopping places. If two readers stopped in the same general area, he concludes it results from *avoidance behavior* caused by his bad writing. Those parts get rewritten.

We have to develop a sense of where our audiences might find the going hard in presentations of our plans—and we have to assume we are creating the problem. It is impractical to find a test audience for a dry run the way the author-psychologist does. There are, however, questions that can anticipate natural resistance to complex and complicated information.

What do our intended audiences already know?

If we tell them what they already know, we are preaching to the converted and wasting their time. If we start with something they know and build to new ideas, then we are using what they know to take them to what we want them to learn.

A common error is to make audiences work too hard. If we are explaining an engineering idea to accountants, we have to find a way of putting the message in terms easy for them to understand. If we are explaining a new accounting procedure to engineers, we have to construct the message in language familiar to them if we want to make it easier for them to understand.

How can we get our message across with the least expenditure of our audience's energy?

Recipes for Boil-Down

We cannot make complexity go away nor can we make simple what is complicated. We can make both manageable by the way we present information. Here are four suggestions for keeping the MEGO score low:

1. *Summarizing.* Being able to summarize content demonstrates a command of it. A summary has the psychological benefit of showing how reducible the content is. A summary is just that: It is not exhaustive but highlights the key points.

> *What are the vital elements of what we want to do?*
> *How can we squeeze them into a single paragraph?*
> *Confine them to a single page?*

2. *Spatial Relations.* If we are putting our plan on paper, we need to think about how it will *look* as well as what it will say. Pages should be designed to allow the reader to track easily through the content. No rule says we must write in paragraphs. If our material has quantifiable elements, we can use charts. If there are key words or phrases, we can make them stand out with visual devices.

> *How do we intend our readers to track through our page?*
> *What can we do to promote the process?*
> *How can we design a summary?*

3. *Features.* There are always special elements to our plan and objectives. Example: If describing marketing strategy for People Express, some of our key words might be *price, destinations and schedules.* We could bury the words in our text or devote a paragraph to each. Watch what happens when we treat them as one line features:

Price. Dramatically lower fares than competition.

Destinations. Many desirable and connecting cities.

Schedules. Wide range of departure options.

By combining the language of summary with the techniques of "features," we say and show what has to be said with a minimum of fuss—and we make it easier on the reader.

> *What features of our plan can be isolated and summarized?*

ASKING "JUST RIGHT" BUSINESS QUESTIONS

4. *Top Sheet/Bottom Sheets*. Our audiences for a strategic plan will have different levels of interest. The financial people may only want to know about budgets and related activities. The marketing people may be more interested in price and availability. Top management may feel it has time only for the "big picture." To satisfy a diverse audience, we can use a top sheet as a summary of the total plan and as many bottom sheets as needed to expand on the major elements contained in the *top sheet*. We hope everyone will read the top sheet and select the *bottom sheets* of interest. (By developing the bottom sheet's first, the top sheet summaries will be easier to write and read.)

• AIMING •
WHAT SEGMENTS ARE WE SEEKING?

Going Privileged Class

At the same time passengers were lining up to get a jump on the best seat locations on a People Express flight from New York to Los Angeles, another group was getting ready to board a plane going to the same destination. This group had been offered a special waiting area away from the riffraff. Once on board, the atmosphere was that of an elegant club: every seat luxurious, more attendants than in the first class of the regular carriers. The setting was created by Regents Air, a name chosen for its connection to royal settings. Regents wanted to make traditional first class look passé. It offered the best champagne, food and fine china. The price made the first class of other carriers look like bargain basement stuff.

To travel in an ordinary jet from New York to Paris takes about seven hours. If in a rush, three or four hours can be knocked off by flying Air France's Concorde, the gull-shaped liner with limited seating and sound-barrier-breaking speeds. Like Regents, it is not cheap. But it is fast.

Regents and Air France identified a segment of the flying population that could be designated "privileged class." Members of the class can afford to pay extravagant prices but the question is: Are they willing to do so in numbers large enough to make rarefied carriers profitable? The decision to make this level of service available was based on seeking market segments representing special opportunities.

Segment Seeking

"Markets" are usually described in broad strokes. There is an automobile market and there is a toothpaste market. But eventually they have to be broken into segments. Buyers in the luxury car segment and its members behave differently from those in the economy car segment. The number of choices of toothpaste includes segments based on taste, tube sizes and special effects (such as paste for super sensitive teeth).

ASKING "JUST RIGHT" BUSINESS QUESTIONS

Whether offering a service or constructing a product, we are seeking a segment:

> *What is the market for our product or service? The most promising segment within that market?*

A useful way of defining a segment is by how buyers will behave. When there was no Concorde to whisk people across the Atlantic, how was Air France to determine whether enough passengers would choose higher speeds at higher prices? One clue was the reception of first-class service. Was it booked full enough to suggest its price was not yet at the barrier levels? What were the hotel and car rental choices' people made? Evidence from actual patterns of behavior suggested the Concorde could be a profitable venture.

Similarly, Regents Air had to examine the routes attractive to big spenders in specific geographical settings. Regents-like service between Los Angeles and Ukiah would not be a likely candidate for plush flying. New York and Los Angeles are the two commercial centers at the right distance for its route to have attractive demographics.

Looking for the Why and How

Among the many market segment indicators, two stand out: *rationality* and *modality*. They are the why and how of market behaviors. In combination they shed considerable light on how segments can be clearly seen.

What is the rationale for flying? In air travel, people fly to get to places fast. If a business trip, someone else is picking up the bill. (Airlines developed frequent-flier programs partly to induce business people to fly certain lines to accumulate points useful for personal travel later.)

How do people choose the modality of flight? With air travel, choices are economy, standard, business, first and luxury class.

> *What reasons would people have to choose our product or service?*
>
> *What modality options should we offer?*

Like Regents, are we to offer only one way to use our services? Or, like Air France, are we offering options?

Is Anyone Out There Listening?

In the 1950s American television viewing habits forced changes in radio listening, making it hard for radio networks to do business as in the past. The survivors made it with less advertising income and fewer production dollars.

Radio made a spectacular comeback by finding segments ignored before television. The reasons' people listen vary enough to help broadcasters discover promising segments. People still listen for the reasons they always did—information, inspiration, entertainment—but within those broad categories are additional slots. Talk shows proliferate. Preachers have used the radio for years, but now they aim at special groups. The portability of radio makes it the most flexible of communication channels.

The modalities are broader than ever. The availability of FM and stereo-FM signals revolutionized radio listening. The mix of program choices and modalities has created a massive sea of segments. There is ethnic radio, high-fidelity radio, all news radio, and so on. The competition from television forced radio broadcasters to develop creative packages for advertisers, such as tying radio to print and television campaigns.

In short, the revival of radio was in the discovery of segments that had always been there awaiting exploitation.

ASKING "JUST RIGHT" BUSINESS QUESTIONS

WHAT IS THE ATTRACTION?

Haute Cuisine and Permanent Waves

What is the real motivation for going to a five-star restaurant? The food? The possibility of being seen with or seeing the rich and famous? Is it being lifted out of the humdrum and temporarily living a fantasy? Is it an experience we seek so that we can say we have been to such-and-such a place?

What about those who own and operate the restaurant? Do they understand the attraction? The chef may believe the whole enterprise turns on the success of his soufflés. The owner may be convinced it is the selection of foods while his or her banker is certain that it is the location of the building.

Restaurants go in and out of business with the regularity of the tides. There is fragility even in successful restaurants.

What is the role of anticipation? The pursuit of an objective can give more satisfaction than its attainment. Men once went to barbershops for haircuts and women to hairdressers to get their hair done. The more successful barbers and beauty shop attendants have since become hair stylists and beauty consultants. Their shops have been transformed into rejuvenation emporia lavishly decorated and overflowing with hair-treatment products ranging from brushes to lotions to sprays, all aimed at making us feel as if we, too, might look like the models in the magazines we read while waiting our turn in the chair.

What is our central attraction?

What role might anticipation play?

What will motivate people to choose us?

Any product or service is bought with a set of buyer expectations. If we understand those drives, we aim to have them fulfilled by our products.

Steam Bath

Before it expanded its vision and changed its name to Baker International, Baker Oil Tool specialized in designing and

• AIMING •

manufacturing oil recovery equipment. From its research, Baker believed its customers would be attracted to customized machinery designed to bring oil to the surface more effectively through viscosity reduction. Its main feature was the ability to send steam down the oil well. Called the Steam Oil Recovery Mobile Unit, it was a technical marvel decked out with instrumentation for monitoring and controlling temperatures, as well as many other features the Baker engineers thought the market would welcome.

Baker understood the need but misunderstood the true attraction. People wanted a simple, inexpensive way to get the steam down the oil well. The extras made the equipment harder to use and more expensive to buy. Since they were not options, Baker had priced the product out of the market. The bath Baker took on the activity steamed its management.

> *How do we maximize the attraction of our product or service?*
>
> *How do we avoid undermining or minimizing the attraction?*

At the beginning of IBM's rapid growth period in the 1960s, it grasped the market implications of data management technology. The technology was likely to change so fast that it would quickly make what was sold today obsolete tomorrow. So rather than selling machinery, IBM leased it. IBM benefited from the true attractions of its data machinery by giving customers the confidence of having the latest models and economical paths to upgrading.

The Look Before the Leap

Market reaction is the best test of attraction. Coca-Cola learned that the hard way: Its research indicated a switch from the hundred-year-old formula would be the sweetener needed to attract the part of the market it was losing to Pepsi and others. But the research never anticipated the strength of the backlash from the loyalists in Coke's established market segments.

There are questions and methods for testing assumptions about attraction before becoming fully committed. To begin with, we

ASKING "JUST RIGHT" BUSINESS QUESTIONS

can ask questions about reliability. Such questioning calls attention to the credibility of the sources asserting our market attraction.

How reliable are our sources?

What is their track record? How sound are their methods? What do our instincts tell us? Do we *trust* them?

How can we verify conclusions?

Can we *objectively* compare the tests done by others with tests of our own? Before being rolled out nationally, many new foods and household products are introduced into test markets to determine reactions in advance. Some products are withdrawn, others remodeled, and successful items put into national distribution. When Sears introduced the Discover card, it was placed in a few major markets to test the card's attraction while outbound telephone marketing polled potential customers in other areas to look for patterns in its market base.

What kinds of evidence will we accept to test conclusions about attractions?

• AIMING •
WHAT ARE OUR RESOURCE ORIGINS?

When Up Looks Endless...

When their horizons burned brightly, what were the origins of the resources of the Mexican government, American farmers, NASA and the U.S. banking industry? Each had its day in the sun. Each operated as if the sun never set.

As far back as the 1930s, a principle aim of the Mexican government was to control its own oil reserves in order to industrialize. It nationalized the oil industry in the 1930s, long before OPEC was a gleam in the eye of any sheik. When OPEC materialized in the 1970s, Mexico saw its opportunity to embark upon an industrialization plan capitalized by loans guaranteed by its oil resources. Cash coupled with its pool of cheap labor presented Mexico with the path from the Third World to the first.

NASA's aim was space exploration. Its resource origin was the U.S. Treasury, by way of Congress, of course. It was helped by a patriotic fervor in the 1960s to be first in space. The aerospace industry, located in politically important states like Texas, California, Florida and Massachusetts, welcomed the new business. Economic objections to a manned flight program (an unmanned program would have been cheaper) were overridden by political considerations.

For most of this century American farmers have had it hard. They are the most productive farmers ever to plow the planet. Their production has outrun our consumption, thus keeping prices low. Agribusiness has been a boon to processors and distributors of food, not its growers. When the value of all real estate shot up in the 1970s, thousands of farmers who had survived low produce prices saw the opportunity to convert their newfound equity into cash to modernize equipment and finally get into better competitive positions. Land, unlike food, is a nonrenewable resource.

The steep inflation of the 1970s caused U.S. bankers to update their thinking. Inflation not only reduced the buying power of the dollar, it also acted as a magnet for foreign investment. Banks created money instruments (certificates of deposit, special funds, etc.) attractive to foreign and domestic investors. Banks were able to raise their interest rates for the new cash and develop new products such as variable rate loans to soften the blow. The resource origins of the banks were the world's available cash.

What are our resource origins?

What does our access to them depend on?

. . .and Down Can Look Relentless

Onto any parade, a little rain may fall. When a market is headed up, it looks as if it will never stop. When headed down, a crash seems imminent.

Mexico believed its resources were in its proven oil reserves. But the resources are dependent on the price of crude. Oil may be a nonrenewable energy source, but if too many countries pump too much at the same time, excess supply drives the price down. Since the to-pump-or-not-to-pump question is often decided by short-term political goals rather than long-term economic strategy, Mexico's resources were connected to Middle Eastern politics and worldwide oil consumption rates. Mexico made its economic forecasts based on $30/barrel crude prices. When crude prices dropped, Mexico's ability to pay installments on its industrialization loans also dropped.

What controls the value of our resource origins?

When an agency lives by public opinion, it can die by it. NASA's honeymoon with Congress and the American people cooled in stages. The 1960s was a period of expansion. Resources were treated as if they were limitless. By the 1970s a reaction has set in, causing resources to be thought of as more limited. A tax rebellion began in bellwether states (California and Massachusetts, long regarded as liberal spenders, voted stringent restrictions on spending) and spread to the national level. The drama of men and women in space lost much of its allure when costs were considered. As space launch disasters and evidence of ineffective administration grew, the space agency looked as if it were just another government bureaucracy mismanaging the public treasure and trust. Cutbacks in the space program—unthinkable in the 1960s—were inevitable in the 1970s and 1980s.

What are the key influences upon access to our resource origins?

All the new equipment the farmers could buy and all the chemicals they could use on the soil could not sufficiently stimulate demand to get the farmers a good return on investment—in spite of a doubling of the world's population since World War II. Starving nations cannot afford American farm products and the American population has not been growing at any rate sufficient to drive farm prices up. The inflation wring-out of the 1980s' forced farm land values down from their highs of the later 1970s' and early 1980s'. Ironically, farmers' resource origins sometimes are inversely related to their agricultural productivity.

What factors might reduce the value of our resource origins?

There is a different irony reserved for bankers: The bigger the debt of the debtor, the fewer the controls for the creditor. When a bank lends a family money to buy a house, the bank can grab the house if payments are not made regularly. Any resistance can be overcome easily. Should the debtor be the Mexican or Brazilian government, however, what can a bank do should the debtor wish to renegotiate the interest rate or renege on the loan? As countries run into domestic problems, they never risk the wrath of their people to satisfy the debt to foreigners. If countries cannot make their payments, they will not risk much in refusing to pay (except the ability to borrow again). For bankers, resource origins reside in worldwide economic conditions, foreign politics, and other factors beyond their control. As inflation is dampened, there is less attraction of foreign cash to American banks. What would happen if American banks were hit by foreign investors taking their money elsewhere if certain foreign governments held back payments on the loans made with that very capital?

What are the commitment levels of our resource origins?

ASKING "JUST RIGHT" BUSINESS QUESTIONS

WHAT ARE THE TRENDS?

Who's Watching the Tube?

For a quarter of a century the three major television networks—ABC, CBS and NBC—thought of their competition as one another. There were small, independent broadcasters in most major markets and there was PBS as a sizable presence, but collectively the competition merely nibbled at the fringes of the mass market. The proof was the Nielsen ratings: The vast majority of viewers divided their viewing time between the Big Three. Each network lived or died by the rating points, with a single point being worth hundreds of thousands of dollars for each chunk of advertising time.

Big Three planners and programmers studied trends of program types, the people and the programs watched (as well as purchasing habits), and one another. Program positioning was vital to the process of getting a handle on viewer demand.

Two events—one legal, the other technical—upset their applecart. To start, cable companies and networks had been springing up all over the country like dandelions after a spring rain. These upstarts had won the necessary legal clearances in communities to string cables and rent services. Many were small, niche players with specialized programs for particular audiences. Others were large new networks such as Fox, HBO and the Turner Broadcasting networks (TBS for general programming and sports, CNN for twenty-four-hour news). Then there were health channels, erotica channels, and shopping channels. Combined, the multitude of channels offered a wide range of alternatives to the mass–oriented offerings of the Big Three.

As if that were not enough, the proliferation of VCRs changed viewing time management: Not only could TV owners record now and play later, they could fast-forward past the commercials. When Nielsen compiles ratings, there is no way to know whether the TV sets are being watched or recorded to be played later, sans commercials.

AIMING

What trends should people in the television broadcasting industry have been watching? What would have told them what they needed to know about changes in viewer behavior and preferences? What trends should they look into for the rest of the 1990s'?

What trends do we watch? What trends have we ignored?
What is the likelihood they will continue?

Surface Trends and Hidden Trends

Hindsight clarifies our view. The fragmentation of the video market was preceded by technical breakthroughs. Satellite transmission of television broadcasts was developed by RCA, NBC's parent before the General Electric takeover. That freed potential broadcasters from having to depend on access to surface transmission and made it possible for someone like Ted Turner to turn a local station into a network base almost overnight.

There were plenty of other signals. Applications for national and local broadcasting licenses were no secret. Of course stations need programs, but they were plentiful enough through the movie studios and old television series whose rebroadcast licenses were retained by the original producers.

Another sign was the emergence of a dominant format for VCRs. Matsushita's success in establishing VHS as the format of choice for VCR owners set the stage for a quantum leap in VCR use because standardized formats result in lower costs.

Finally there was a pattern in the use of prerecorded cassettes. VCR owners were viewing over fifty cassettes a year, but instead of buying, they were renting. What would happen if video purchase prices decreased? If more cassettes were bought, TV sets would become multi-use systems: broadcasting would no longer be the single use of a set—and less time would be spent watching broadcasts.

There are signs that now familiar videocassettes will be replaced by CDs with more information and greater accessibility. When widescreen TV sets come on line with better

ASKING "JUST RIGHT" BUSINESS QUESTIONS

picture quality, consumers will have a staggering array of choices. Among them will be network TV, but it will play a smaller role in viewer choice.

In considering trends, we need to ponder those that support and potentially undermine our long-range planning.

> *What trends support our ideas?*
>
> *Which could be supported by developing technical breakthroughs?*
>
> *What trends are unsupportive of our ideas?*
>
> *How crucial would the discontinuation of a trend be to us?*

• AIMING •

HOW CONDUCIVE ARE THE CONDITIONS?

Inside, Outside

If the trends favor us, how could the conditions be anything but favorable? To start, trends are signals of changes in conditions. People may be changing habits and technical developments may still be some distance away from creating new realities. Conditions are the broader contexts of the society and worlds in which we have to function.

If we look at conditions inside,

What is the attitude of top management?

Words of encouragement are welcome, but more convincing are the level of resources and attention giving support to what we are trying to do. How much time has top management given to us? What resources?

How important to top management is our project or plan?

When we look outside at the broad conditions, there are five critical concerns:

How supportive are the economic conditions?

Asked the secret of the stock market, J.P. Morgan said, "It fluctuates." When looking at economic conditions, we need to think not only of how they are but of how long they will stay in place.

How does the competition affect conditions?

As long as IBM stayed out of the personal computer market, expansion was easier for Apple Computer. The entrance of IBM was a recognition that the personal computer market had all the aspects of growth that attract large and small players.

What cultural reactions are likely?

If we are introducing a new brand of shoes, there will be no cultural ripple—unless the intended market had always gone barefoot. As the motion picture industry became more daring in frank language and bare skin, it ran into resistance from various regions and philosophies.

ASKING "JUST RIGHT" BUSINESS QUESTIONS

What psychological consequences might there be?

There was a time when people were repelled by hygiene products being shown in plain sight in drugstores. The 1960s' paved the way for psychological acceptance of these products in display racks next to aspirin and shaving cream. Psychological consequences carry the potential for a backlash: People offended by a product might stop coming to the store and might try to keep others from doing so.

What legal considerations should be analyzed?

Ours is a litigious society. Ambulance chasers are the least of a modern organization's possible headaches. There are safety, trademark, copyright, and a veritable lawshelf-long list of violations or alleged violations that a simple act of development or promotion can bring down on our corporate head.

As we survey conditions, we can get better control over the many variables by asking about the rate of change in the conditions and which conditions are most important to us:

How fast might conditions change?

What are the crucial conditions for us?

Up, Up and Away!

When Lockheed made the decision in the late 1960s' to build the L-1011, the conditions could not have been more supportive. Inside, top management was anxious and itching to get back into the commercial airplane business. Outside, all systems were go. There was a ready market for the size, speed and glamour of the L-1011.

But then Lockheed encountered competitive and economic problems. The L-1011 had to go nose to nose with McDonnell-Douglas's DC-10. A market Lockheed expected to have to itself became highly competitive. The engine designer and manufacturer for the L-1011 was the prestigious Rolls-Royce. Formidable problems with materials and pressures to meet deadlines for engine delivery were so insurmountable that Rolls-Royce went bankrupt. It could not deliver the engines and, consequently, Lockheed could not deliver the planes.

· AIMING ·

By mid-1971 Lockheed was on the brink of disaster. By a one-vote margin, the U.S. Senate gave Lockheed the loan guarantees needed to stay alive. As for the L-1011, it had a fifteen-year life at Lockheed during which it was unprofitable, distracted and drained top management, and kept them from turning to other ventures.

What preparations can we make to cope with supportive conditions going sour?

ASKING "JUST RIGHT" BUSINESS QUESTIONS
WHAT SPECIAL FACTORS INFLUENCE OUR BUSINESS ENVIRONMENT?

Connecting with the Variables

Once we have a fix on the trends and conditions, we need to ask questions about those factors peculiar to our industry or market segment. Consider: The economic recovery of the 1980s included better conditions in the overall energy industry excluding the nuclear energy segment. Special factors affect that segment. Unless someday resolved—the nuclear segment will not follow the industry trends.

What factors are peculiar to our industry?

If we were in the book publishing business, we would be part of the larger communications industry. Special factors confined to book publishing are the cost of paper, postal rates (for companies involved in direct mail marketing), and the health of book outlets.

The popular business book, *In Search of Excellence*, emphasized the roles of managerial expertise but ignored the factors of the business environment. Those factors were later decisive in the fortunes of the excellent companies described in the book: The state of the economy, business cycles of diverse industries, technological changes, and governmental policy changes were among the key variables that changed in the early 1980s. Changes in the business environment undid some of the managerial "expertise" presumed responsible for the achievement of excellence. (For a discussion of how *In Search of Excellence* missed the environmental factors, see Daniel T. Carroll's essay, "A Disappointing Search for Excellence," in the November/December 1983 *Harvard Business Review*.)

How concerned are we with our special business environment factors?

Format Wars

Technology has spawned several electronic publishing boomlets that have gone bust. When videodisks first appeared,

• AIMING •

RCA and Phillips each tied its fortunes to a particular form. RCA developed a needle system for "reading" the signal on the disk, Phillips a laser beam. The presence of both blocked a standardized format—and that in turn kept the market from establishing a base of playback equipment on which videodisks from any maker could be played. Instead of taking off in the consumer market, videodisks became confined to industrial and archival functions. The competitive factors represented by the two disk technologies reduced the possibility of a large consumer market.

Matsushita Electric Industries—known more familiarly as Panasonic through its product lines—understood the need to clarify and deal with standardization in its business environment. The market Matsushita confronted was divided into three videocassette formats, the older $^3/_4$-inch and the newer VHS and Beta $^1/_2$-inch types. Matsushita was not concerned about $^3/_4$-inch because it believed the high expense would make that format unattractive to consumers. But it was worried about Beta, developed by its arch rival, Sony, because most technical experts considered Beta superior in picture quality.

Matsushita and Sony understood that if the market favored one format, it could become the standard and wipe the other out. Sony promoted picture quality by way of educating consumers. Matsushita approached other VHS equipment manufacturers with attractive offers to build the insides of their brand-name products at reduced prices if they would take the VHS route. Matsushita understood that when VHS machines dominated the consumer market, VHS prices would fall and turn *price* into a decisive factor within the videocassette business environment. There were other factors for Matsushita: standardization, customer acceptance, ease of use, and so on. All were dependent upon price, not picture quality, as Sony believed. By 1986 VHS sales were outrunning Beta by ratios as high as 11:1. VHS has since become the standard.

What are the decisive factors within our business environment?

ASKING "JUST RIGHT" BUSINESS QUESTIONS

Four Factors Worth Watching

There are generic areas peculiar to any industry to ask about: government policies, technological changes, financial realities and the responses of competitors. Each varies within business segments, so the answers to look for have to be specifically tailored to our market.

In the United States, there was strong support for governmental regulation of business from the 1930s to the 1970s. Every major industry had to consider the factor of policies and regulation. Some industries, such as oil, were able to get favorable treatment through lobbying. A decisive shift to deregulation began in the Carter presidency and accelerated during the Reagan and Bush administrations.

Deregulation, however, unleashes special consequences, as the airline and railroad industries have so painfully learned. Whether regulating or deregulating, the role of government has to be considered. That role is not limited to what happens in the White House or in the halls of Congress. In a globalized marketplace, there are foreign governments to consider, especially when so many products are multi-national in derivation of parts and in the possibilities of markets.

What governments, and what government policies, affect our business environment?

Every change in the technologies supporting our particular business has potentially enormous consequences for us. Matsushita has won the VHS-Beta contest, but now there are new battles to come. Compression technology, a fiber-optic and/or wireless information superhighway, mergers between Baby Bells and broadcaster, the potential for computers and TV sets to work together in startling new ways are some of the technological changes that will dramatically alter the communication industry.

What special technologies does our industry depend on?
How might changes in them affect our environment?
How might we better manage this?

• AIMING •

Financial realities are always with us. Existing short- and long-term interest rates are never guaranteed. A change in accounting practices can turn red ink into black or black into red. The ways companies account for payments into retirement funds can make financial performance look better than it was. The choice to downsize may improve overall productivity but demolish performance of parts of a business.

> *What financial factors carry special significance in our environment?*

How well do we know our competition? If we introduce a new item or service, raise or lower a price, what response might competitors make? Is our industry segment free of a dominant organization or is it one where the pygmies operate in the shadow of a single giant? What will change by one company mean to the others?

> *What are the likely competitive responses to what we do or might do?*

ASKING "JUST RIGHT" BUSINESS QUESTIONS

WHAT CONSEQUENCES ARE WE SETTING IN MOTION?

Living with the Pandora

Had Pandora known what was in the box, would she have taken the lid off? Was there no clue? In the airline industry, how might established carriers anticipate the cutthroat price competition? Experience may teach us much but it cannot teach us everything. We may think we understand how an event triggered consequences in the past, but that event was in a time and place that has undergone change. Therefore a manager is never able to predict every consequence set in motion by his/her actions. All we can do is watch for unforeseen consequences as well as those anticipated. We can train our sensors to pick them up early—looking for negative and positive fallout patterns externally and internally.

How do we speculate about consequences?

Where do we look and what do we look for?

Accentuating the Positive . . .

When the market for commercial information management equipment was growing, IBM salespeople found a hungry market for IBM products and services. Seeing an opportunity for rapid expansion, IBM's management found a creative response to the consequences: Territories were cut in half and quotas were raised. At first there were howls of protest from the salespeople. Was this any way to treat a successful sales force? It certainly was. With smaller territories and additional salespeople, there was less time between calls, more quality time with customers, and more time to find new customers in the smaller territories. The salespeople made more money than before as IBM turned positive consequences into even more positive results.

How could we capitalize on positive consequences?

... Eliminating the Negative ...

Whenever a new concept is introduced into an organization, there is a high potential for distraction. There may be resistance that is inevitable when humans are faced with change. There are no simple formulas for making things easy from the start or getting people to embrace change warmly. Those are bridges to be crossed—and anticipated:

> *How can we anticipate negative fallout from what we have set in motion?*

Naturally the solutions have to wait for the problems to occur. Asking about the possibilities in advance can reduce their impact and our reaction time should they occur.

... and Dealing with Those In-Between

The court rulings eliminating "ownership" of athletes by professional teams came when the revenues from professional sports were rapidly climbing. The major sports moguls were signing lucrative TV contracts, being pursued by cities desiring franchises, dealing with massive sports complexes with complicated contractual obligations. By no longer owning the players, the dynasty building by the richer franchises ended. The turnover rate of personnel became subject to free market forces in ways never before experienced by sports management, but the enormous contracts have not been a guarantee of outstanding performances.

One set of consequences provides new opportunities for franchises to be successful. Another set of consequences has subjected owners to a new set of rules for managing their resources. Some of the old families historically associated with baseball have had to sell out because they could not compete. Others have jumped in, some successfully and others with disastrous results. The successful owners (the Toronto, St. Louis and Los Angeles franchises, for example) have made the adjustment to the "new rules."

> *What consequences are likely to be the most complicated to manage?*

ASKING "JUST RIGHT" BUSINESS QUESTIONS

This chart of questions, which is not intended to be exhaustive, suggests the range of consequences to ask about:

	NEGATIVE	POSITIVE
INTERNAL	What is the distraction potential? What resource competition will there be?	What growth opportunities are being created? What new applications of our resources might there be?
EXTERNAL	How aroused will our competition be?	What expansion opportunities are occurring? In products? Markets?

Why Stop with Labels?

When Prohibition ended in 1933, distillers such as Hiram Walker and Seagram's went back into business in the United States. They had been aware of the importance of labels to the buyer's decision-making process in liquor stores and needed to reassociate themselves with label manufacturers in the United States. It was a specialty printing business. Special paper stocks had to be selected. Machinery for cutting, printing and embossing labels was an expensive import. Much needed to be known about adhesives that could secure labels to bottles without coming through the image side.

Theodore Fleming and Harley Potter started a printing business to serve the reestablished liquor industry. For years it prospered, adding distillers over time. Its biggest problem was dealing with the consequences of success: expanding fast enough to keep up with demand.

In the 1960s management passed to the second generation as Ted Fleming, Jr. took over. Looking west from his corporate headquarters in Peoria, Illinois, Fleming offered label services to the wine industry in California, then at the start of its meteoric expansion. In studying his new clients' needs, Fleming discovered that wine-makers imported their wine-making equipment from Europe. Since Fleming already imported sophisticated machinery from Europe, he established a new business, wine-making machinery importation.

Coupon printing is a close cousin of label printing. Fleming started printing coupons for manufacturers of cereals who used them in their boxes to sell other products. The cereal makers had problems getting enough coupons in enough boxes fast enough. Putting coupons in boxes could consequently slow down the delivery of the finished product. Fleming, who already had engineers on staff to repair his printing presses, turned his attention to the custom design of coupon insertion equipment, a new product for Fleming Packaging.

ASKING "JUST RIGHT" BUSINESS QUESTIONS
WHO ARE OUR AUDIENCES?

Spectator Sports

Who are the audiences for professional sports? Clearly the folks inside the stadiums are an audience: Attendance records are kept with the same eye for detail as are the numbers kept to track every nuance of recordable activities on the field. Professional baseball teams were once content when a million fans showed up in a season. Now that mark is below the break-even point. Three to four million in a season is a realistic goal of the successful franchises in markets like Los Angeles, New York, Toronto, Denver and Miami.

On-site attendance figures pale when compared to television audiences for a sporting contest. Seventy-five million sets may be tuned in to a World Series or Super Bowl game. One regular season game may draw as many viewers as an entire season's on-site attendance.

Television executives and advertising marketers are very sensitive about the kinds of commitments the baseball establishment asks for broadcast rights. In one of the early contracts between baseball and NBC, the baseball owners made a long-term commitment without any upside protection. It cost them dearly when NBC viewership went up for its "Game of the Week" program. NBC paid a flat fee to baseball and raised its advertising rates. Since then baseball has bargained hard, as has football. Both sports have redesigned their games to fit the needs of television: The two-minute rule, the limits on visits to the pitching mound, and other innovations were designed to quicken the pace and add excitement for TV audiences.

A decisive audience for the sporting establishment is advertising executives who deliver the sponsors. Large crowds at televised games are convenient props for the television crews—especially if there are dull moments during a contest. If the crowd contributes to the spectacle being televised, the TV revenues may be more significant than gate receipts.

• AIMING •

There are baseball and football executives who once believed that local TV coverage would hold down attendance. Most now realize that it stimulates attendance over the course of a season.

> *Who are our external audiences? What do they have in common?*
>
> *What are the significant differences?*

There are internal audiences as well. In our organization there may be layers of top management with general and specialized interests in what we are doing. A New York Yankee who misplays a ball in a televised game may have more concern for the reaction of George Steinbrenner, the well-known majority stockholder of the Yankees, than for how his fan club will react to the miscue.

A common managerial error is to treat all internal audiences as if they were one. They are as different as their organizational functions:

> *Who are our internal audiences?*
>
> *What are the major differences between them?*
>
> *How can we best communicate with each internal audience?*

Keepers of the Gate

"Gatekeepers" are people who can facilitate or block a message intended for someone else. When we have our final audiences in mind for a communication or product or service, we should ask about any other individuals or groups performing gatekeeping functions. Parents can keep a child from viewing an undesirable program. An affiliated station may not carry a network show. Reviewers are gatekeepers. What they write about books or movies, or don't write about them, influences public reaction.

> *Who are the gatekeepers between us and our final audiences?*
>
> *What special handling might the gatekeepers require?*
>
> *How does the decision-making done by gatekeepers differ from that of other audiences?*

ASKING "JUST RIGHT" BUSINESS QUESTIONS
WHAT ARE THE READINESS LEVELS?

How Ready Is Everyone?

In analyzing what it takes for people to learn difficult subjects, professional educators try to discover what foundations have to be in place before understanding can occur. If young children are to learn to read, questions of their readiness levels must first be raised: Do they understand that printed letters stand for spoken sounds? Do they realize that English goes from left to right and then top to bottom?

The readiness levels of our audiences need assessment—both the internal and external audiences. Within our organization there may be different levels of understanding of what we are doing. Externally our prospective markets may have different levels of interest—or disinterest—in what we are telling them. Our ability to get our message across to any audience depends partly on an audience's needs and partly on our ability to package our message to address those needs. If readiness levels differ, what does that do to our packaging?

What are the readiness levels of our different audiences?

What do the levels have in common?

What is peculiar to each audience?

If we are making automobiles, the engineers will have a different level of understanding about how things work than most of our external audiences. As we address the question of how the car works, the approach we use in explaining it should be adjusted to each group's readiness level.

Our audiences may be even more unruly than a captive class of five-year-olds rebelling at the suggestion that the initial sound of the word *one* is not represented by the letter *w*. Like all audiences, our audience is bombarded by messages trying to capture their attention. The issues for us are how to attract attention, hold onto it, and take it where we want it to go.

Have we primed our audiences?

• AIMING •

Why would any of our audiences pay attention to us? What is in it for them? What preparations can prime them?

At the start, the management at People Express understood it had two major audiences, employees and customers. Both could be attracted by different treatments of the same content: *We are a discount flier asking you to make some changes in the way things are done to reach economic advantages.* Employees were hired on the basis of owning a little piece of the action in exchange for doing their jobs differently from their counterparts at other airlines. Customers were solicited on the understanding that putting up with a little hassle could save a lot of bucks. Both audiences needed to display a readiness to make changes from past practices.

Starting Up

In new ventures, questions about the readiness levels of audiences are crucial, especially when they relate to matters of resources, time and the acceptance by both organization and markets.

What is the readiness level for the long haul?

As television helped drive the expansion of professional sports, the start-ups of new franchises required long-term staying power. If key people expected results faster than was achievable, the whole enterprise might be doomed from the start. But if management was ready to stay the course because it had been readied for the course's length, the prospects for success improved.

When the New York Mets baseball team was started in 1962, the strategic plan called for a team to be put on the field immediately to establish a franchise, while a farm system was set up to feed players to the top and build a championship team. No one was sure how long the process might take—indeed, if it would even work. The 1962 Mets set records for dubious distinctions: They lost more games than any major league team before or since. The team was a collection of over-the-hill veterans and cast-offs whose glory days were behind them. Managing the menagerie was Casey Stengel, himself a cast-off from the Yankees because of his advanced age. (He was prone to snoozing on the bench during a game.) While everyone laughed, more serious matters were happening in the farm system. Many talented scouts were signing and developing the likes of Tom Seaver and Nolan Ryan. The seedlings came into full bloom in 1969 when the team won the pennant and the World Series. Seven years from start to payoff.

Management was gratified but not surprised. It had been primed to understand the time needed to develop young athletes into major league stars. The people in charge of the farm system—the organization's major resource—were developing new talent. To give the idea time to work, the strategic plan included provision for building the right readiness in the right people.

· AIMING ·

WHAT IS THE PROCESS FOR OBJECTIVES EVALUATION?

Bulls-Eye . . . or Bull-Only?

This *Aiming* chapter opened with an image of a marketing manager drawing a circle around a dart after it had been thrown. The answers to the strategic questions should prepare us to draw some circles so we can start throwing some darts.

Why circles? Why not Squares? What size should they be? How far away? What is their source?

How do we develop criteria for evaluation?

What is the process? Who is involved? At what stages are various players involved?

Who and what determines the evaluation process?

The idea of objectives in management has been around long enough to become a vital process in some organizations and a ritual in others. Being evaluated on the basis of performance objectives can be a serious business or an annual chore delegated to clerks who copy last year's set for this year's submission.

What are the connections between our objectives and our strategy?

How serious are we about objectives as our evaluation criteria?

Do our objectives accurately describe what we want to happen? What are the consequences of failing to meet them? The rewards for exceeding them?

When the New York Mets were started, the Payson family (the original owners who later sold the franchise to the Doubledays) understood there would be a long period before profit objectives could be met. The obvious objectives were winning games and drawing crowds. Less obvious, but fundamental to the establishment of the club for the long haul, was how future prospects were developing in the minor leagues. The objectives set for that part of the operation were crucial and as long as they were being met, management could tolerate the misplays of their major league players. The circles drawn on the walls of the front office showed how well youngsters were learning their craft in the minors.

Compared to What?

Evaluation means comparison. The basis for that comparison is a crucial decision for an organization. There are at least three possibilities: past, planned and potential.

1. *Past performance* has the virtue of simplicity and the drawback of simple–mindedness. Comparisons with the past can draw inordinate attention to how we once did rather than the conditions, trends, and environmental factors at work when we did it. If we compare past and present performances without also comparing the enabling circumstances, we will mislead ourselves. If New York Mets attendance is up or down from last year, might it not be related to how the other New York team—the Yankees—is doing this year and how well it did last year? Comparisons with the past make sense when past and present conditions are alike.

> *How similar are our present conditions to our past conditions?*

2. *Planned performance* moves the criteria closer to the present. When we compare actual performance to planned performance, the burden falls on how well we planned and executed.

> *How have we built our objectives into our current plan?*

3. *Potential performance* asks about possibilities. The Mets of the early 1960s' had no possibility of becoming a better club—unless management looked beyond the field to players of the future.

> *What objectives can measure our potential?*

Changing the Objectives in Mid-Stream

As we travel farther from the time our objectives were established, internal and external changes may occur to alter their feasibility. Conditions and environmental factors may have become so supportive that our objectives, drawn seriously, are aimed too low. At the other end of the spectrum is the tendency to promise more than we can deliver or be pressured to do so. The question is how adequate the objectives remain:

> *How do we adjust the evaluation criteria to important changes?*

Do we have to wait for the next annual review of objectives? Have we built into our strategic planning the mechanisms of review to keep the objectives connected with what is happening?

> *How do we change objectives in midstream without undermining the evaluative process?*

Using the Evaluations

Evaluating performance can be used as the basis for rewarding or punishing. Used that way, the value will be limited. If our objectives are seen as just another version of the carrot-and-stick philosophy of management, the ability of people to "beat the system" will emerge.

The lasting value of evaluations is change and growth. Each session for developing and evaluating our objectives should be done in the spirit of finding answers and reaching our full potential both as individuals and as an organization. The evaluation of objectives becomes an important means to improving performance, not an end in itself.

> *How do we use the evaluations of our objectives?*

> *What does the evaluative process mean to the individuals involved? To the organization?*

ASKING "JUST RIGHT" BUSINESS QUESTIONS
WHAT ARE OUR STRATEGIC OPTIONS ?

Big Blue and the Little Apple

We are now at the end of the *aiming* stage. It is time to ask ourselves what our reactions will be if we are not where we plan to be by the time we have planned to be there:

If we find we are not on schedule with our plan, what will we do?

This way of thinking attempts to anticipate problems before they confront us—and to take advantage of unforeseen opportunities should they occur. In other words, terms such as *options, alternatives* and *contingencies* need not apply only to worst case scenarios. They have as much worth when put into action in response to best case scenarios, too.

To begin, we need to build into our evaluation processes a continual examination of the strategic options open to us. When IBM entered the personal computer market, it hitched a strong computer to a weak keyboard. The market response was positive to the computer, negative to the keyboard. The speedy appearance of a new keyboard from IBM suggests that it was hoping the first keyboard would make it, but was ready with an option if it did not.

IBM's entrance into the home market shook up Apple. For a long time IBM was content to dominate the commercial market and Apple was pleased to have the personal market. When IBM changed its strategy to pursue the home market as well, it was typical how IBM had used its strength: The option had been there all along. The real issues were timing and readiness.

Apple Computer's response was ill-conceived and rushed. Apple tried to make its computers attractive to the commercial world. It asked salespeople skilled in the personal computer markets to do a quick change into supersalespeople in markets they were not prepared to enter. Had that been a preplanned strategic option, there would have been the proper preparations for a move so drastic. Instead, Stephen Jobs brought in John Sculley for his marketing skill. Later, with full board approval, Sculley squeezed Jobs out because of Jobs' lack of marketing options.

Refreshing or Recycling?

How do we build strategic options in advance?

Admittedly it is difficult to get the creative juices flowing about what to do *if* this or that should happen. People already committed to a strategic plan have to be convinced that the plan is not really ready to go operational unless viable options have been thought through. We have to get everyone to see that a plan without workable contingencies is like a car without a reverse gear: The gear may not be used much, but it must be there for those times when a major change in direction is called for. Alternatives should be fresh ideas, not rejects from another time and place:

How do we generate strategic thinking that is fresh and potentially challenging to our existing strategy?

What would we do if a new option sounded better than the original plan? Could it be that IBM came up with the improved keyboard as a result of thinking of alternatives—and that what it did was speed up the production when the market reacted badly to the original keyboard?

If nothing else, consideration of genuinely fresh strategic ideas keeps the organization's cerebral processes active and sharp. It is a way of staying in shape. Like the rest of our organs, we have to use them or risk losing them.

The Contingency Mindset

In the Epilogue of this book mention will be made of the mosaic mindset, an ability to see the connections and chain reactions of what we are doing and might do. That state of mind is needed for considering strategic options:

How will the total plan change if certain strategic options are put into play?

How will existing tactics be affected?

ASKING "JUST RIGHT" BUSINESS QUESTIONS

If we are not where we said we are going to be, where will we be when the full effects of a strategic change are in place?

Change the Strategy or Tweak the Tactics?

The corporate landscape is littered with the corpses of those who confused the failure to reach a strategic objective with the need to switch the strategy. Whenever we are ahead or behind our plan, we need to begin with a line of questioning to determine whether our attention should be on our strategy or our tactics. Apple Computer's reaction to IBM's entry into the personal computer market was a strategic response but a tactical one would have been better advised. Apple had a sizable lead over IBM and excellent market standing. Rather than working from its strengths, Apple worked from its weaknesses to attack IBM's strengths.

What would have happened had Apple avoided the commercial market and fine-tuned its tactics in the personal market to combat IBM?

> *How can we be certain that a strategic option is better than a tactical change?*
>
> *A tactical change better than a strategic?*

One clue is whether we are acting out of intimidation, jubilation or deliberation. Apple was clearly shaken by IBM's entry into the home market. Panic may have led to the decision to go into the commercial market. Coca-Cola hoped it could get away with the formula switch, but when an important segment rejected it, Coke management had a tactical option ready, not a strategic one.

Banana Republic started as a mail order marketer of high–style khaki. The response was so strong that it was able to increase the frequency of its mailings (a tactic) and open up stores nationally (a strategic response) when its market responded enthusiastically. If the response was purely from jubilation, opening the stores could be a drag on success. But if opening stores was a strategic option originally built from a "what if we are really successful" scenario, then its thinking flowed from a solidly based plan.

Timing and Consequences

Finally, whenever we make important changes, we have to time them to minimize the adverse consequences and maximize the advantageous. Sears, Roebuck's ability to compete with aggressive discount retailers has been hampered by an internal distribution system no longer suitable for today's marketplace. Sears reorganized by reducing its number of regions and removing an entire layer of management between the top and operational levels. It did so at a time when housing starts were dramatically up, a traditionally good market opportunity for Sears. Sears' strategic options included internal reorganization to allow it a better external position. A more recent strategic decision to discontinue the Sears Catalog, arguably an internal reorganization option, has implications that reach into the *Conceptual/Seeing* area (What is our identity?).

> *If we need to use any of our options, what would the best timing be?*
>
> *Other than the desired consequences, what else might happen if an option were activated?*

ASKING "JUST RIGHT" BUSINESS QUESTIONS

Chapter 3
DOING

It was to be the tallest building ever—so tall it would reach to the heavens! Construction brought together engineers and workers in such good spirits with materials in such abundance that completion was certain to be within budget and ahead of schedule.

There was one hitch. In a nutshell: God objected to an invasion of His air space. Thus it came to pass that He caused everyone to babel in different tongues, so gumming up the works that the tower was never finished. Moral: *Unless operations work, creative visions and great plans come to nothing.*

ASKING "JUST RIGHT" BUSINESS QUESTIONS

WHAT ARE OUR TACTICS?

From the Strategy Come the Tactics

Answering questions about the business we are really in and the strategy we intend to pursue are the table-setters for asking about tactics. Although we have to be prepared to reconsider earlier answers about our business and its strategy, the likelihood of our strategy changing is small in comparison with the chances for tactical change. Therefore, not only do we want to know what our tactics are, we want to know when and how to change them. We start by seeing the connective tissue between our established strategy and our current tactics:

How do our tactics support our strategy?

How frequently do we review tactics?

Keep the Strategy, Change the Tactics

When Coca-Cola saw its market share go into a decline, its alarm grew because of the implications: Research clearly demonstrated the younger consumers' preference for a sweeter, more Pepsi-Cola-like flavor. Since early soft-drink preference later turn into brand loyalty, Coca-Cola feared for its long-term strategy: domination of the soft drink market.

Coca-Cola did not rethink its strategy. It changed its tactics. It carefully studied market demographics, conducted taste panels, and finally concluded a dramatic tactical change was in order. For the first time in nearly a century, Coke decided to alter the unalterable: Change the formula!

The hoopla surrounding the historic decision must have gratified Coca-Cola management. Media attention acted as a supplement and reinforcement to the massive campaign mounted by Coca-Cola. Unfortunately for Coca-Cola, all of the attention exacerbated the resentment of old Coke diehards. Their reaction made Coke's new tactic turn out the way a carbonated can of soda does when shaken: fizz in the face.

• DOING •

Once again Coca-Cola changed tactics. This time Coke did it right: Turning the backlash to its advantage, Coke corrected its first tactical error by resurrecting the original formula as Classic Coke and keeping the Sweeter version as New Coke. Old customers got what they had always wanted and Coca-Cola was able to pursue new customers to stem the loss of market share.

Coca-Cola may have come in for a great deal of second-guessing from marketing and advertising people, but through all the turning and twisting, Coca-Cola never lost sight of its central strategy. Each move Coke made was a tactical maneuver in pursuit of its strategy. The tactics changed as quickly as the conditions.

What would cause us to change any tactics?

How long would the time lapse be between recognizing a need for change and being able to make the change?

Coating a Tactic with Plastic

Sears, Roebuck's decision to bring the Discover card into a crowded consumer credit field raised many eyebrows. Was it going head-to-head with the likes of VISA and MasterCard? Did Sears think it could compete with American Express?

To understand the tactic, we need to look at the Sears' strategy: From its early days, Sears' strategy was expansion of what a retailer could offer its customers as their needs evolved. Sears moved with its markets and the times—and in many instances anticipated where the market was headed. Long ago it offered catalog services to people too far away from stores for convenient shopping. Times changed and so did Sears when it saw the new opportunities in the construction of massive stores to serve the growing number of affluent buyers in the suburbs. Sears always made it easy to acquire goods by choosing moderately priced products and offering credit terms. It sells installation services. It sold insurance for years through acquisition, entered the real estate and financial services industries.

The Discover card was a tactic to keep up with its market. It expanded upon financial businesses it was in and gave its customers another financial option.

How do our tactics evolve?

How do our tactics confine our strategy?

Sears problems in the 1990s stemmed from more efficiently run discounters like WalMart. Sears did not properly attend to its core business, retail sales. It grew too many management levels and may have entered too many related businesses. At this time, Sears appears to be getting back on track by shedding some businesses and better management of its retail business. The Discover card has become established as market presence for consumer credit.

Strategy in the Light of New Tactics

As Coca-Cola discovered, understanding the dynamics of a fundamental market change is no guarantee of a correct tactical choice. If the new tactics we design do not work, what does that suggest? Are our tactics faulty or is our strategy stale?

When does tactical failure signal a need for strategic review?

When we are in the *doing* phase we resist even the suggestion of a strategic problem. For Coca-Cola there was no reason to think of its strategic goal as unrealistic. Any tactical failures were just that, a need for course corrections, not a need for a new map. For Sears, however, reversals required a new strategy.

When does tactical change signal strategic review?

• DOING •

WHERE ARE THE BOTTLENECKS?

Send in the Bulldozers

Doubleday & Company, a major publishing concern, pursued the paths of vertical and horizontal integration in its publishing activities. It owns bookstores, a direct mail operation, and even its presses—very unusual in an industry served mostly by outside printing firms. By owning its own presses, Doubleday takes lower manufacturing costs and converts them into better profit margins.

In the fall of 1979 Doubleday could do no wrong. It had bought a couple of small publishing houses, had more than its usual share of best-sellers on its fall list, and was enjoying the demands of bookstores clamoring for more copies. Doubleday increased its print runs to keep up with demand. At this time Doubleday installed a new computer system to keep print runs, bookstore orders and inventory control running smoothly. It also did some top managerial reshuffling.

Everything worked independently but nothing was coordinated. Books showed up at the warehouse faster than they could be absorbed. At first the excess was temporarily put in the aisles of the warehouse. While managers tried to find places for the books that had arrived, more books kept coming until there was no room for them inside the building. In the meantime new orders kept coming from the booksellers, stimulating more press runs. Out of desperation, old books were bulldozed out of the way to get at books needed to fulfill orders. Millions of dollars were lost in what Doubleday insiders described as the Great Warehouse Disaster.

Seeing Where the Critical Steps Lead

In developing the Polaris missile program, the U.S. Navy came up with a quantitative method for figuring out what steps were needed, how they overlapped, and how much time each one required. It became known as PERT, or the Program for Evaluation and Review Technique. In the language of PERT, a *critical step* is one requiring completion before succeeding ones can start. When the critical steps are aligned in the "technological sequence," they can be plotted along a network called the *critical path*. Had Doubleday made a critical path of how new books would move from their printing facilities to their warehouse storage locations, one of the critical steps would have been to make room for new books before they arrived. Space availability was a critical step whose completion was required before new books could sensibly be received. The failure to plan for the books' arrival was a failure in understanding how their own systems would work when activity accelerated.

Some Japanese and U.S. manufacturers have applied critical path thinking to a more efficient and effective way to turn over inventory and cut carrying costs. They have fine-tuned the delivery of certain components from suppliers to the point where the materials are not received until they are actually needed in the assembly process. Perhaps someone asked why certain components, that are never in short supply, should be stored at all? Or, whether suppliers could deliver on a schedule convenient to us rather than to them? If the plant managers know at what point on a critical path they will need specific items, why not get them when needed rather than before?

> **What is the critical path for our plan or project?**
>
> **What critical steps can we focus on to avoid a bottleneck? Exploit an opportunity?**

Stepping Out

Some of Doubleday's woes could have been avoided by isolating the *enabling* steps in the chain, beginning with the ordering of print runs and ending with shipping dates. An enabling step is one that must be completed before several other steps can take place:

> **What steps, if not completed on time, halt the subsequent chain of events?**

Examples: Space has to be available in the warehouse before books can be received and then shipped. The computer system needs to be coordinated among the warehouse, the order department and the printing facility.

It pays to look at *supporting* steps as well. A supporting step is not vital to the process, but it can facilitate it. If there is a master plan to coordinate the critical steps, people can be alerted to the problems before they occur.

Stepping In

Clearly seeing steps is half the battle. The other half is managing them. An excellent plan managed badly will not work long, unless we are more lucky than smart.

> *Who will be responsible for getting the critical steps accomplished?*

Whether a committee or a person is in charge, there must be some way to be sure that after the critical steps are identified, they are integrated:

> *What will be the integrating force assuring us the chain of events will hold together?*

Keeping the Process Moving

When everything is humming, there is a tendency to relax. The day *before* matters started to unravel at Doubleday might have been the right time for a review. Since no system is ever perfect, and because we operate in dynamic environments, systematic review is itself a critical step:

> *How frequently should our critical steps be reviewed?*
>
> *How detailed should reviews be?*

ASKING "JUST RIGHT" BUSINESS QUESTIONS
WHAT KINDS OF MANAGERS DO WE NEED?

A New Era, a New Style

In the industrial era, Henry Ford and John D. Rockefeller epitomized top management. Although they might not have characterized it this way, what they sought in managers was strong *convergent* thinking styles. A convergent thinker is one who can funnel information into a narrow focus. If the "big picture" is already established, as it was at Ford and Standard Oil in their heyday, then managers were needed who made the little cogs go in the big machines. If problems arose, their solutions were likely to be found in experience. It made sense to have employees come up through the ranks. Corporate loyalty was valued and rewarded over the long haul.

The industrial era is giving way to the post–industrial age, a time suited to *divergent* thinking styles. This is the ability to take seemingly unrelated events and see new relationships in supporting what an organization does or may be doing. Analytical power may be valued over experience. What an employee can do for us now is more important than what has been done in the past. The rate of change in the postindustrial era moves faster than it did in the industrial era.

The way managers approach problems may be more indicative of how they will perform than their track records suggest because the problems of the future may have few direct corollaries with the past.

> *What management styles are best suited to what we do and will be doing?*
>
> *What styles will allow us to develop the skills we want managers to have?*

New Times, New Managers

In the late 1960s Lockheed was an industrial giant of the post-World War II period. The word *multinational* was not then in vogue but if it had been it would have described Lockheed. It sold jet aircraft to the resurging industrial countries of the world. The engines for those planes were purchased from the British engine and automaker, Rolls-Royce.

It all unraveled in 1971. When Rolls-Royce went bankrupt, Lockheed panicked. How to acquire the jet engines in time to meet the many contractual deadlines became an obsessive dilemma.

Lockheed, once high and mighty, was soon up against the wall. What had worked so well for so long was headed for a crash landing. Many steps were taken by Lockheed's leadership to get into the air again. One decision involved the kinds of managers it now needed. Lockheed understood that although it had been successful with managers whose styles once meshed with an era fast disappearing, the time had come for a new style. The very kind of manager who had made Lockheed successful (authoritarian, aggressive, task– and power–oriented) was now causing it to fail. A replacement program rather than a retraining program was put into place because Lockheed asked itself about the best ways to develop the managerial skills it now needed. The managerial styles it had relied upon were not conducive to the new skills it was going to need. Lockheed instituted early retirement programs and started looking for new-style managers who were supportive, assertive, achievement– and relationship–oriented.

What is the management style that has distinguished our successful managers in the past?

How will the style work in the future?

Structure and Style

By seeking a new managerial style, Lockheed's leadership took a chance that its own structure might not accept the change easily. It was a "chicken-or-egg" dilemma:

What do we change first, managerial style or organizational structure?

If our organization has been geared to one type of managerial style, what happens when a contrasting style is introduced?

ASKING "JUST RIGHT" BUSINESS QUESTIONS

How adaptable is our structure to the managerial styles we seek?

If we are imposing new styles on an old structure, what will happen if new managerial styles run into blockades within our structure?

How adaptable must managers be to the organizational structures in place?

If we change too much too quickly, we run the risk of imposing chaos where there was order:

How do we balance organizational structure and managerial style?

The creatures of the Galapagos Islands were on Charles Darwin's mind when he observed that survival depended on adapting to whatever hand evolution dealt. Had Darwin studied modern corporations, he might have invented an adaptability index to measure the ability of an organization's structure to survive its managers' styles and for the managers to survive an organization's intransigence:

What is the adaptability level needed by the managers we need?

By the organizational structure we have in place?

Personality as a Clue to Style

Personalities can be rechanneled but cannot be substantially changed. If we want clues about how a manager is likely to handle matters in the future, we need to ask questions about the dominant personality patterns the manager carries as part of his/her psychological baggage. At the extremes of managerial styles, there are four psychological patterns worth knowing about. We need to be aware that it is rare for any person to consistently behave in a fashion associated with only one trait. It is more likely to have elements of at least two of the four traits. What we look for are tendencies and dominant combinations, especially in the contexts of the decision-making process.

AUTOCRATIC	BENEVOLENT
An issuer of orders, dictatorial in style	Unilateral in style but softer in delivery.
PARTICIPATIVE	CONSULTATIVE
Requires consensus before making decisions.	Seeks views of others in making decisions.

In the full flowering of the industrial age, a manager with a mix of the autocratic and benevolent would have been well suited to the assembly line mentality. The issue was not how to do the jobs differently, it was how to do the jobs faster. In a post-industrial setting, the ways jobs are done keep changing. Therefore, participative/consultative styles of management are more likely to work best.

What personality traits are supportive of the managerial styles we need?

How will we identify them?

ASKING "JUST RIGHT" BUSINESS QUESTIONS
HOW DO WE MAINTAIN CONTROL?

Looking for Ground Truth

Aware that vital information can become distorted by passing through too many filters before getting to the top, military commanders learn to ask,

How do we get ground truth?

They are not looking for truth ground up like hamburger but for the information to help them to make the right decisions in the midst of a battle. They must be sure the information they receive is as free as possible from the embellishments and protective coatings it might get on the way up.

In management we need to have controls plugged into the critical areas of what our organization does. There are questions about the information itself, what we do with it, and how we transmit it:

What is critical data for us?

Is it actual sales figures compared to projections? Productivity indices? The "vibes" we get from walking through an operation?

What kinds of inferences can we make from our critical data?

How do we extrapolate from the information we have? (It did not take Coca-Cola long to see what the withdrawal symptoms would do to its market base.)

What does our transmittal process do to information?

Inadvertently or intentionally, the medium can muffle the message. What are our means of communicating critical data?

Formal and Informal Controls

The formal controls are easy to spot. They are the numbers with the most meaning. They may be sales reports, schedules, percentages, exchange rates or some other quantifying mechanism. In a world dominated by science and technology, "the numbers" offer evidence of whether what we are doing is working.

Alongside those numbers we need to consider informal controls. They are the vital signs of an organization's health we can get by "walking around." If attitude, esprit and morale are telltale signs, how do we aim our antenna at them?

> *How do we supplement our formal controls?*

Do we spend time in the field or do we bring people in the field into the home office? If we rely on reports, how do we read between the lines?

> *What are our informal controls?*

Management Information Services and Disservices

It is hard to find an organization without some form of owned or rented information services. The common name is MIS, or management information services. Hardly a week goes by without a new service possibility arising from expanded computer capacity or new software designed to give managers more printouts to read. We need to know the roots of the reports and the angle of vision of the report makers. For instance, if our MIS operation was originally installed for inventory management, it is possible that when asked to expand its attention to marketing analysis, MIS will try to pour marketing needs through an inventory sieve. In many organizations MIS got its start as an extension of accounting and financial needs. There may be built-in biases preventing that sort of MIS history from properly responding to the needs of research and development.

> *What was our original purpose in starting an MIS operation?*

> *How can MIS help us build the controls we need now?*

The Controls at Chrysler

When Lee Iacocca took over Chrysler, he looked at four vital signs of a company out of control: *Inventories* were bloated. Chrysler's manufacturing activities were not synchronized with its sales. *Labor costs* were soaring as if driven by a supercharger. This cost factor kept Chrysler from having a competitive edge against foreign manufacturers. *Staffing* was out of balance. There was a disproportionate number of managers when compared to labor and corporate needs. *Market analysis* was in paralysis. Forecasts were contributing to the inventory glut. Chrysler was headed for the scrap heap.

Iacocca took actions in each of the areas of need—and was able to monitor the effects of his actions by keeping an eye on the control mechanisms. He lowered prices and watched his inventory numbers head down. He reached an accord with labor, thereby getting those costs closer to the levels Chrysler needed to become competitive again. Middle and upper managers were let go until the management/labor ratios were in line with industry standards. Marketing reports were made on the basis of the ground truth of market behavior and not on the basis of protecting anyone within the organization.

> *What are our vital signs?*
>
> *How do we monitor them?*

Contrasts in Controls

At the height of Apple Computer's success under its founders Jobs and Wozniak, Peter Drucker predicted neither man would last. The prediction was based on his observation that neither had sufficient operational experience to be sensitive enough to the possibility that things might get out of control. Being so successful so young may have contributed to Jobs and Wozniak not having developed either the right sensitivities or controls. The second generation of leadership at Apple was Sculley, a man more in tune with the market changes of the '80s because of his marketing background. Now in the '90s Sculley is replaced and Apple is seeking greater current understanding.

> *What are our attitudes about controls?*
>
> *When and where were our attitudes formed?*

At the other end of the control spectrum was Harold Geneen, the ITT Chairman who doggedly and steadily built sales from $766 million to $22 billion dollars. He claimed to look *behind* the numbers. He subdivided his massive organization into over

250 profit centers—and kept a book on each. The books went everywhere Geneen went. He had one way of reviewing them on a weekly basis, another way for a monthly review. Whenever something caught his sharp accountant's eye, he made a phone call (even in the middle of the night) or convened a meeting. Geneen looked for *deviations*—not just danger signs, but positive signs as well. A danger signal indicated a need for a change in plans immediately. A success signal suggested to do more than what was being done. Geneen was committed to a certain level of growth for every quarter, and he knew what controls to look for to stay on top of his organization. The harsh style of execution became unacceptable but he was right on the understanding and importance of controls.

> *What would tell us whether we were in or out of control?*
>
> *What do we do and how do we do it when we find a need for action?*

ASKING "JUST RIGHT" BUSINESS QUESTIONS
HOW DO WE ACHIEVE POWER INTEGRATION?

Integrating Power

In World War II the allies struggled to achieve massive cooperation from groups that were historically competitive. Although they faced a common enemy bent on their annihilation, the past histories and future aspirations of the American, Russian, British, French and Chinese leaders led to petty bickering and deeply divisive differences. Having power is one thing, using and distributing it for common goals if another.

It was all symbolized by the planning of the Normandy invasion. Not only did different nationals have to be under a single command, service rivalries within the countries had to be overcome. Traditionally the navies, armies and air forces are under separate commands and wary of encroachment from each other. The invasion of Europe required the naval forces to carry the ground forces and, with the air forces, provide cover. What made the most sense: A military management committee? A supreme commander? If the latter, was he to come from the navy, army or air force? What country should the leader come from? An American leading a European invasion? A European symbolizing unity? The answer, General Dwight Eisenhower, with an elaborate Allied staff, is obvious now, but it was neither obvious nor inevitable then.

Distribution of, an accountability for, power are only simple when an operation is small enough to be concentrated in one pair of hands. On that scale, everyone knows where the buck stops. When operations grow, the buck makes lots of stops. The power is spread. Some stays at the top, much is dispersed "below." (The notion of "top" and "bottom" comes into question when those at the top realize the degree of reliance upon those at the bottom.) As the power dispersal begins, we should consider what happens in the process:

What mandate accompanies power grants?

If we hold people responsible for a task, are we giving them power commensurate with the responsibility? If we are giving or

• DOING •

getting power, what degree of responsibility goes with it—and is it understood by the giver and the getter?

> *How do we know the power mandate is clear to all the participants?*
>
> *The power givers? The power receivers?*

Establishing Responsibility and Extending Power

Responsibility begins where the action is. For over thirty years General Motors built assembly plants whose designs were solely the responsibility of those at the top. For years complaints coming from the bottom had a familiar ring: Assembly–line workers said they could have done a better job of designing the assembly–line operations had they been involved. Those sentiments were largely ignored and unknown to the outside world until workers at the Lordstown assembly site in Ohio revolted. Fed up with being held responsible for completing tasks they felt were made harder to do by the design involved, they refused to accept responsibility any longer until they were granted some power over the lines they worked.

Times have changed. The GM Saturn plant in Tennessee, departed from the GM mold that created the Lordstown confrontation. GM has come to understand the value of participation—and that those who have responsibility also share in the power.

> *In assigning responsibility, how do we extend the power to discharge the responsibility?*

We can delude ourselves by thinking the act of assigning a task carries with it the necessary power and responsibility to get that task done. Unless the extension of power is clear, such assumptions may get us into trouble. We have to work at making sure we all understand the power grant:

> *How do we communicate a new grant of authority?*
>
> *What are the likely reactions?*

Clarifying the Authority Structure

Delegation of authority runs the risk of unintentionally undermining the authority structure. When analyzing tasks to determine the powers needed to accomplish those tasks, we do not necessarily intend a change in the authority structure (unless, of course, that is an objective). By delegating and sharing power, are we inadvertently sending a message that we are surrendering power? Or that we want to be out of the decision-making loop? What will change after transfers of power and responsibility? As we change the power structure, we need continual review of the implications:

> *How clear is the power structure after we delegate power?*
>
> *What is our clarification process?*

Highflying Power

People Express's initial strategy was to offer frequent flights at permanently low fares. As a competitive edge, it sounded good. To make it happen in an industry already overcrowded and deregulated was not so easy—especially when the established carriers had the resources to sustain losses in extended price wars. And where to cut costs? There could be no diminution of safety standards, no way to purchase aircraft more cheaply, no new routes to introduce. The answer was in leasing aircraft, acquiring distressed airlines, and asking how passenger services and support systems could be reduced without driving the passengers away.

But the pay-for-what-you-get policy did not cut enough costs. People Express had to reduce labor costs and recognized an opportunity to change the established carriers' tenured staffs with salaries inflated by years of service. To justify it, People Express gave labor a stake in the company and, with it, a rationale for accepting extra responsibilities. Instead of specializing the jobs of the ground personnel—the folks who check in and otherwise process the passengers—People generalized the jobs. Someone who checked passengers in had other jobs to do as well, based on needs as they occurred. To get workers to accept increased responsibilities, decision-making power and encouragement in the taking of initiatives was extended and communicated. Workers were "empowered."

· DOING ·

The objective was to get as many passengers on a flight as quickly as possible. It was in everyone's interest—"top" management, "bottom" management, and the passengers. What's more, everyone knew it: Passengers were thought to be less likely to gripe about the frenetic boarding at a People departure (when compared to the more orderly ritual at the traditional carriers) because they were getting a bargain—an example of the customer willingly sharing in the meeting of a corporate objective. Everybody would win because everybody would benefit.

At the operational levels power and responsibility were integrated with each other *and with the objectives of the corporate plan.* By having employees share profits and power, productivity was to rise and fewer people were to be needed.

In contrast, the traditional carriers had been more rigid in parceling out power to employees. Until deregulation, traditional carriers could pass through higher labor costs to ticket purchasers.

Lack of competitive forces resulted in few questions about lower costs and competitive prices. Deregulation changed that. The bargain carriers, like People Express, forced this issue:

> *Do we have an environment in which our people our empowered?*
>
> *What are our productivity benefits if we integrate power differently?*

ASKING "JUST RIGHT" BUSINESS QUESTIONS

HOW DO WE STAY IN THE HERE-AND-NOW?

Reconstructing the Past and Dreaming About the Future

A CEO sensed a serious problem in his organization. He intuited that it could make his entire organization come apart. He held meetings with different managers. He tried walking around the company to better acquaint himself with the views of those well below his level. After a time, the problem was clear. He gathered his key staff in the boardroom and announced, "I completely understand the problem—and I do not wish to ever deal with it again." Having seen the here–and–now, he wanted it to go away.

A scary present reality can cause people to look elsewhere for relief. The past is one place: "If we had only done such-and-such, then everything would be all right now." The future is another safe haven: "This is a learning experience. Next time we will do it right." Psychologists describe these reactions as *avoidance behavior,* attempts to dodge present reality by dealing with something else. As children, we get early training in the art of avoidance. As managers, we have to recognize the symptoms in ourselves and in others in order to stay on top of what we are trying to do.

What are our initial instincts when we get bad news?

Do we look for others to blame? Do we construct explanations of how we got to the sorry state: Do we construct scenarios of how things will get better later? If we try to escape the present by the stratagems we learned as children, we should ask:

How do we overcome avoidance behavior?

Here-and-Now Orientation

We begin by looking at how we describe immediate reality. If we use a *prescriptive* approach, then we trap ourselves into thinking about what ought to have happened—and avoid what has happened. Prescriptive thinking is suitable for post-mortems and future planning, but for dealing with immediate needs, it falls short.

• DOING •

If we take a *descriptive* approach, attention is focused on what is going on right now. In some training seminars and programs for managers, a here-and-now simulation exercise is experienced to demonstrate how to avoid avoidance behavior. Two of the rules for problem-solving are worth noting:

NOT ALLOWED: *The participants can neither refer to anything in the past nor in the future.*

ALLOWED: *Action plans must be stated in the present tense and describe what is to be done right now.*

What would happen in our organization if we imposed those rules on a problem? In the *doing* phase we have to keep reminding ourselves of the need to stay with present realities.

> *What are the signs of a healthy here–and–now orientation?*

Here–and–Now Maintenance

In his heyday at ITT, Harold Geneen held full-dress reviews of objectives every month. The meetings were mandatory and convened the heads of all of his more than 250 profit centers. If one of those centers fell behind its objectives at any time in the fiscal year, everyone heard about it and was asked for recommendations at the meetings. Geneen was especially sensitive to any signs of being behind early in the year: He did not want his managers to delude themselves into thinking there was time enough to turn matters around. He wanted action then and there.

There was a threefold purpose to the meetings: First, they acted as an early warning system for any center headed for trouble. Second, they were a reminder to all present of the consequences of falling behind early or late in the year. Rationalizations were unacceptable, action plans were the only course to pursue. Third, they alerted everyone to success stories and enabled Geneen to increase whatever activities were contributing to exceeding objectives.

Geneen's methods seemed harsh to some of his critics. None, however, deny that the methods worked. Since his objectives were shared by his managers—and since the payoffs for success were well above industry standards—the methods paid off for the organization and its successful managers.

What will work for us? Quarterly reports? Weekly meetings? Retreats? Study groups? Quality circles? What are the ways we employ to rivet attention on the here–and–now?

How do we maintain the here–and–now?

When Reality Changes

In Theodore Levitt's famous essay, "Marketing Myopia," mentioned earlier, he contrasted railroad and airline management's perceptions of reality in the 1930s. The railroaders derailed themselves from future growth by not understanding they were in the transportation business, not just the railroad business. The airline executives could see how to position themselves as transportation providers, an understanding that led to dominance of passenger transportation years later.

Just as reality changed for the railroad companies of the 1930s, reality changed for the airlines of the 1970s. The deregulation of the 1970s was preceded by ample warning. Few of the companies were ready for the degree of route competition, merger activity, and upstarts like People Express. Like clear air turbulence, a need for here-and-now orientation descended on the traditional carriers because reality had changed.

Knowing what is about to happen will not automatically help us avoid it, but it can help us take steps to anticipate it. If there are defects in the parachutes, it is better to know before we jump.

How alert are we to the way current realities reflect fundamental changes?

Part of the here-and-now process relies on adequate feedback, an area we will return to later in this chapter.

How in touch are our feedback systems with reality changes?

· DOING ·
WHAT IS REALLY GOING ON?

Figuring Out What Is in the Brew

Concerned with a sharp rise in accidents, a large brewery hired a consultant to develop a safety program. The company had been owned and operated by the same family for a couple of generations. It was paternal in its managerial style and rewarded by a high degree of employee loyalty. Manager and managee alike wanted something done to improve safety in the workplace. The consultant's job was thought to be to institute a safety program.

Before developing safety measures, the consultant asked questions about morale, equipment and safety records at competing breweries. Worker morale was high, the company's equipment was the best available, and yet other breweries had better safety records. What accounted for the difference?

One important difference between the brewery's employee benefits program and its competitors' was that workers, thought of as part of the extended family, were allowed to sample as much beer as they wished. It was one of the better beers and it was free, so some workers simply drank more than they could handle. By the end of the workday some were sloshed enough to make errors dangerous to them and costly to management.

Now it all looks perfectly clear. But at the time what management saw was a climbing accident rate to be corrected by a safety program. The employees who took advantage of the generosity offered them may have been too bleary-eyed to make the connection. Neither saw what was really going on.

Causes versus Symptoms

On-the-job alcoholic intake was the cause, accidents were the *symptoms*. When trying to determine what we need to do about a problem we have detected, we should consider what we are really witnessing:

What are the symptoms and what are the causes?

ASKING "JUST RIGHT" BUSINESS QUESTIONS

In any organization there can be personality conflicts. A common conclusion is that "the chemistry" is wrong or that "communications are poor." Suppose there was a conflict because two managers had overlapping areas of responsibility. What we might see first is the squabbling and infighting—the symptoms of overlap, not the problems of chemistry or communications. The cause is an organizational matter. If the combatants were transferred to other departments and replaced by new people, the same problems would probably occur because the cause had not been changed.

When we hear of internal problems whose simplistic causes have been identified, we can test the prevailing wisdom:

What are the dynamics of what is going on?

What historic rivalries have there been?

There are traditional disputes between marketers and makers of products. When there is vast product acceptance, the marketers take the credit from the makers. Being at the point of the sale, they can make a strong case. When a product is running into a wall of rejection, the makers blame marketers for a failure to find the market. And so it goes.

Looking at the dynamics of situations requires looking beneath the surface. It is like the difference in understanding the intricacies of the plot of a great book and comprehending what is driving the plot's action and motivating the characters. To identify what happens next is not as complicated as being able to figure out why it happens.

When change is introduced, problems may follow whose symptoms may be easier to see than their causes. People asked to change a familiar activity may rebel in ways not even clear to themselves. They may come to work late, be inefficient where they used to be efficient. What has changed? Have they changed or have we changed what they do?

What is different now from what used to happen?

Changes Beyond Our Control

So far we have confined questions about what is going on in areas within our control. But when there are unexpected market shifts or environment changes, asking what is really happening gets at core problems. At first the leadership at Coca-Cola saw a fundamental taste trend strongly suggesting a change in its formula. Management thought the change was what the market wanted, that it knew what was really happening "out there."

Wrong. It was not a market shift, it was market fragmentation.

What market fundamentals should we watch?
Environmental factors?

Looking for Icebergs

Distinguishing between a block of ice and an iceberg comes partly from experience. It also comes from systematic surveillance of the waters we navigate. Managers need to preserve enough objective distance from an operation to maintain a healthy perspective.

What are our provisions for having broad-based perspectives of operations?
In what ways do we get fresh perspectives on our markets?

The brewery that wanted a safety program needed help from the outside to see what was happening on the inside. (There was no change of generosity to employees, just a rechanneling of it.)

At Coca-Cola the leadership could have met the resistance to the loss of the old Coke by doing more advertising for the New Coke. Pepsi would have liked that. Coca-Cola looked harder at its market and, like the brewery, found out what was really going on.

HOW DOES OUR COMMUNICATION OF OBJECTIVES TAKE PLACE

Nailing the Word to the Wall

Imagine the reaction in Babylonian villages when officials showed up with Hammurabi's Code in their carts and nailed it up for all the citizenry to see. Until then—about four thousand years ago—laws were what the kings, queens and their close associates said they were. Whatever prompted King Hammurabi to take the trouble and expense of writing them down and hanging them up is not known, but it could have been in response to the following:

What is the best way of communicating our objectives?

or

What is the most effective way of communicating in our organization?

We have more options than Hammurabi did: He could have held outdoor meetings but he did not have the voice amplification systems we have. We can write our communications down just the way he did, but we can duplicate them faster and in greater numbers than he would have dreamed possible. We can talk by telephone, by E-mail, and by FAX to people in other towns and continents. All things considered, Hammurabi used the most effective means then available.

How effective are we in communicating important objectives?

The Communications Transaction

Whether he intended it or not, Hammurabi's innovation of writing down his code invited feedback about it. What he did with the feedback (or to the people who gave him the feedback) is unknown. When we are spelling out our objectives, we need to consider what kind of feedback we want and what we will do with it when we get it.

• DOING •

What are our preparations for feedback on our objectives?

When we are building a feedback loop into the process of communicating objectives, we are involved in a communication *transaction*. This should not be confused with a *negotiation*. When negotiating, we are giving and taking. When transacting, we are opening the doors to two-way communications in which reactions are solicited. The control is still ours, and so are the opportunities to improve both the communications and the objectives. We should focus our questions about what promotes communication:

How much consultation is needed between those formulating the objectives and those implementing them?

When implementors are asked to take part in the formulation process, new ideas may evolve. The Japanese "quality circle" promotes that idea and is a vital part of how management opens up the communications transaction.

Once Again, Style

If we widen the communication loop, we need to be mindful of our communication style and how well it fits with two-way communications. Earlier we noted there are four pronounced managerial styles related to personality structures. (See page **121**.) Those same traits show up in our communicating styles:

AUTOCRATIC	BENEVOLENT
Controls the message, the podium and the audience.	Controls the message, and the podium but listens to the audience's reactions
PARTICIPATIVE	CONSULTATIVE
Constructs the message with the audience until consensus is reached.	Sends the message and invites active feedback from the audience. Chance for message to change.

ASKING "JUST RIGHT" BUSINESS QUESTIONS

Hammurabi probably had an authoritarian style: "Here is my Code; get with the program." If he used a consultative style, it was confined to his queen and advisors: "What do you guys think about my code?" A participative style in his day and age would have been as likely as Colonel Muammar el-Qaddafi checking out proposed changes in the law with Libyans. Sophisticated managers are best served by a range of styles, each suitable to the objectives and intended audiences.

> *What communication style best assures commitment and implementation?*

Saying What We Mean—and Being Sure Others Hear What We Say

Looking at it now, Hammurabi's Code is simple. It was a distillation of the laws of the land and the code of conduct handed down from earlier generations. Whenever anything is boiled down that way, it may be clearer to those drafting it than to those trying to understand and live by it. The American Constitution is another example: The framers thought they had a clear picture of what they were trying to communicate. Two centuries later what they meant is still debated.

For managers concerned about communicating objectives, attention needs to be paid to what is being heard, not just what is being said:

> *What level of clarity is needed by the audience?*
>
> *What degree of specificity is needed?*

Clarity and specificity are critical. The writers of the Constitution had a concept of equality on their minds, but after two hundred years it is still being defined. Knowing what we mean is never enough. The test is whether others know want we mean.

> *How clear are our objectives to those who have to carry them out?*
>
> *How will we know when they understand?*

The answers to questions like these are unknown until performance demonstrates understanding—or lack of it. When

• DOING •

objectives are initially communicated, there is an opportunity to save lots of steps by actively pursuing feedback. That calls for a consultative or participative transaction and maybe a change in communication style, especially if the communication of objectives is important to our plan and its implementation. In a world where more and more activities are done through delegation and cooperation, the level of communication is critical.

What happens if our objectives are not communicated adequately?

ASKING "JUST RIGHT" BUSINESS QUESTIONS
HOW WILL WE SECURE COMMITMENT?

Monkeying Around with Commitment

We do not wish to suggest that monkeys in a cage are similar to people in the workplace. Still, monkeys *are* distant relatives. Psychologists like to demonstrate the effect of too many bananas on too few monkeys by first training monkeys to perform an operation in exchange for a reward, like a banana. When the monkeys catch on, they are happy to perform as long as they are sufficiently hungry. Increasing the banana supply at a time when the monkeys have had their fill of bananas will not motivate the monkeys because they will be sleeping off the bananas already consumed.

Too much too soon may have been the problem for an affiliate of the American Broadcasting Company in the mid–1970s. ABC's Nielsen ratings, which determine what advertising time is worth for national and local users, were then consistently lower than for NBC and CBS. The affiliate, located in the San Francisco Bay area, was not only tied to the network's poor showing, it also had to compete with another ABC station in San Francisco whose broadcast range overlapped the affiliate's territory.

The station's owner and manager hit upon a scheme to secure the commitment of the sales managers to increasing sales. The idea was to increase salespeople's commissions and to remove any cap on what could be made. Surely the prospects of vastly greater earnings would secure their commitment?

Did it ever? It also came at the time ABC turned its fortunes around with innovations like "Monday Night Football" and other aggressive, imaginative programming ideas. Up went the Nielsen ratings, carrying with them the time charges for national and local advertisers. The effect on the income of the sales managers was spectacular. The money rolled in so fast and in such stupendous sums that the sales managers' incomes surpassed those of the station owner and manager. Instead of being spurred on to greater heights, the salespeople turned their attention to what to do with their new wealth. More time was focused on real estate investments, mutual funds, and tax shelters than on how to maintain the business. They had received too many bananas too soon.

Aligning Commitment and Payoff

Commitment is a word whose meaning has been dulled through too much use and too little definition. In the *doing* stage it refers to how much involvement there is by the people we are asking to carry out the organization's objectives.

When an operation has become mostly routinized because of years of practice, the commitment levels are easier to spot. In those circumstances the problem is not so much getting commitment as it is keeping commitment:

How do we maintain commitment over the long haul?

In start-up situations, the way people are introduced to what they will be doing can set in motion how well they will respond.

What do we offer—and what do people want—to ensure a smooth launch for a new endeavor?

Whether start-up or ongoing, we must pay attention to motivation:

What kinds of motivation lead to full and continued commitment?

At the ABC affiliate, the answer "money" was too simplistic for a problem so complex. Commitment and payoff have to be aligned in ways that ensure continued productivity, unless everyone will be satisfied with short-term results. Commitment over the long haul can be bought with money, but it has to be accompanied and modified by career growth, a suitable working environment as well as perks and incentives an organization can offer and afford. It comes down to a two-edged question:

What are the payoffs? For whom?

The payoffs have to be for both the people whose commitment we want to secure and for the organization for which we all work. If it gets one-sided, everyone will lose. A capless incentive program, like that at the ABC affiliate, paid off only for the

ASKING "JUST RIGHT" BUSINESS QUESTIONS

salespeople, not the organization. Securing commitment has to benefit the entire organization.

Commitment Style

Communication and commitment styles are as related as Siamese twins. A practitioner of the autocratic/benevolent style may get lip–service commitment to objectives. That superficial commitment will last as long as the "leader" is credible and the "followers" are afraid.

The consultative/participative style requires a leader who can get people to voluntarily share a vision and agree to work toward it. Many leaders project their zeal in contagious ways. Once the contagion is caught, will it remain? The conditions promoting commitment are crucial if the commitment is to be permanent. If those conditions depend only on a leader's zeal, what will happen when the leader is off doing something else? Real persuasion occurs when a change takes place in someone's view of his/her role and the accompanying payoffs.

Commitment secured through negotiations is the hardest to accomplish and the longest to last because we are giving something to get something. The ABC station manager gave away the store to save it—but he did not get enough in return to justify what he offered. Genuine negotiation involves participation by all parties to the agreement. Everyone is giving and getting. If everyone shares the vision of how meeting objectives benefits the organization and its membership, chances are improved for productive involvement by the people whose commitments we need to attain the organization's objectives.

Staying the Course

We have cautioned that commitment obtained is not the same as commitment forever secured. Compare the commitment strategies of Lee Iacocca and Harold Geneen. Geneen had to convince his top-level managers that ITT could grow at an annual rate of 10 percent no matter what happened to the business environment and without regard for business cycles. He wanted them committed to that growth goal, which was the objective of those famous monthly meetings to review progress and to search out areas in danger of falling behind. He claims to have paid his top executive at least 10 percent more than the industry standards, but he acknowledged everyone's excitement at being caught up in a heady experience as the reason so many stayed so long.

Iacocca had to convince people that sacrifices were needed to save jobs and Chrysler, but if a ship is sinking, why would the crew trust the captain—especially a captain who has just boarded? Iacocca had to persuade some managers to stay and to get unions to participate in the elimination of jobs. As charismatic as Iacocca was, his vision of a healthy Chrysler had to be coupled to what it would mean to those who remained. The plan he proposed had to be negotiated with those charged with its implementation. It had to be their plan as well. Indeed it had to be the Chrysler Plan, not the Iacocca Plan.

How do we secure commitment for the long haul?

ASKING "JUST RIGHT" BUSINESS QUESTIONS

HOW DO WE HANDLE ROLE EXPECTATIONS?

Quality Eventually Counts

During the worst times of the 1970s oil shortage, there were a few automobile owners who waited in no lines and filled their tanks whenever they pleased. They drove diesel-powered automobiles, all made in Europe, where diesel engines for passenger vehicles had been common for years.

Seizing the opportunity, General Motors rushed to market with diesel engines grafted onto the gasoline engines of top-of-the-line models such as Cadillac and Oldsmobile. There was no time for extensive research and retooling. The press of market demand was real. Buyers were willing to pay a hefty premium for the diesel option, a charge offsetting any fuel cost savings represented by the then considerably cheaper diesel fuel.

By 1984, however, GM had withdrawn from the diesel market. The trade-in value of those cars they had made was nil. The withdrawal resulted from a market being badly burned by inferior quality in design and assembly. General Motors settled a class action suit brought by outraged diesel owners by offering cash settlements or gas engine exchanges.

The lack of quality resulted from the role management imposed on engineers and assembly–line workers who responded accordingly: The emphasis was on getting cars out as fast as possible. A quality watchdog would have slowed down output.

Compare that kind of role expectation with what happens at Mercedes-Benz, one of the successful builders of diesel automobiles. Quality is truly "job one" throughout Mercedes operations. An assembly–line worker can reject a part or turn back a car being assembled in the knowledge the decision will be fully supported by management. Mercedes workers have described a feeling of being spiritually connected to the automobiles they work on. Mercedes' prices—especially in North America— are high. Yet demand seldom flags for the cars and purchaser satisfaction polls demonstrate great loyalty. Mercedes does not need slogans about the "pride being back" because the pride was never allowed to leave. Mercedes creates an expectation in its people that they are there to ensure a level of quality that will make them the best in the industry. It is not a slogan, it is part of the way the strategic plan articulates the vision. It is exactly like IBM's commitment to quality and service: It starts as a vision, becomes part of the strategy and is embedded in every level of the operation. People expect to play their roles and derive satisfaction from doing so. At GM, the role expectation was bound up in how many automobiles a day could come off the assembly lines. It, too, was part of a strategy and gave satisfaction to those employees who found ways to speed up production. (How satisfied they were when GM had to get out of the diesel business is another story.)

> *What are the role expectations we create?*
>
> *How do the role expectations support our strategy?*

The Roles People Play—and the Payoffs They Expect

Once above subsistence levels, salary takes a lower place on the ladder of job satisfaction factors. Money can be surpassed by needs for autonomy, self-worth, accomplishment, potential for growth, and contributions to a "higher good."

Being a priest, for instance, provides satisfaction in doing the work of the Deity. But what of being a customer service representative? Sometimes the biggest lightning bolts are saved for the first available service "rep." During Prohibition, a "revenuer" may have found satisfaction in enforcing the law and stamping out Demon Rum—and dissatisfaction in getting shot at by an unsympathetic moonshiner trying to make a living.

What are the payoffs for doing unpleasant tasks? For a file clerk it may be getting an entry-level position in the hope of climbing the corporate ladder. In creating role expectations, we need to show people how performance is connected to payoff.

> *How is performance connected to payoff in our operation?*
>
> *How achievable are the payoffs?*

A Note on Fit Perceptions

Every manager faces the problem of how to find the best compromise between fitting a person to a job and a job to a person. A judgment has to be made about how an individual's skills, talents, interests and experiences will fit with organizational requirements and objectives for a job. Expressed as role expectations by both manager and managee, we can arrive at a situation where both know what is expected.

The level of involvement of the managee in that process is changing in our post–industrial world. Oddly enough, an Old World organization like Mercedes-Benz is better equipped to instill role expectation in workers which satisfy them and meet corporate objectives. A New World giant like General Motors is relearning how to do that.

The more workers are involved in creating expectations for themselves, the better it is for management. Their perceptions of how they fit in and the process leading up to the perception need close attention:

What is our way of establishing role expectations?

How involved are the people who are being asked to play the roles?

• DOING •
HOW DO WE ACHIEVE PRODUCTIVITY?

Japanese Do It an American's Way

Essentially, what we get for what we give defines our *productivity*. Ingrained in our thinking is the idea that to get more—raise productivity, that is—we have to give more—pay more money, hire more people, buy new equipment, and so forth.

However, experts believe in a technologically based world, using more resources does not necessarily result in increased quality—and with it an increase in productivity. One of these experts was W. Edward Deming (1900–1993), an American statistician who spent most of his career demonstrating the compatibility between higher quality and lower costs—and the lack of inevitability of higher costs leading to higher quality. He proved that a genuine organizational commitment to increasing quality can lower costs and raise productivity. Examples: an organization paying bonuses to people making useful recommendations about cost cutting and product improvements; people at operational levels advising management about kinds of equipment needed for greater efficiency. Deming demonstrated that when given the chance, workers can show management how to get more from resources already owned.

His ideas took a long time to be embraced in the United States. The major reason was the requirement to involve workers at input and judgment levels higher than top management has been accustomed to. In Japan his reception was another story. Each year the Japanese award one of their companies a prize for best alteration of performance standards to achieve higher levels of productivity. The award is called the Deming Prize.

Pursuing Productivity

How happy are we with our productivity levels? What might we do to raise productivity? Is our answer always involved in spending more money to get better results?

> *How might we raise productivity without increasing expenditures?*

The Deming answer is involved in thinking differently about how we utilize what we already have:

> *How can we use existing resources differently to raise productivity?*

In the early 1980s Ford Motor Company came up with its Alpha Project to reverse the company's quickening slide into oblivion. Until then, its automobiles were getting painted with a reputation for poor styling and uneven quality. The Alpha Project aimed at overhauling the way things were done and the kinds of products to be manufactured. Assembly–line workers were consulted abut quality steps. Designers were given freedom to come up with automobiles whose performance would make a difference in the marketplace. Some of the resulting lines resembled Mercedes-Benz in appearance while their promotion called attention to the lower Ford price. Ford regained its financial health and customer satisfaction led to brand loyalty.

Performance Standards

To improve productivity, we have to examine the importance of performance standards. The components of a performance standard are *time, money, quality* and *quantity.*

How much time can we afford to consume on any part of a job? Deming showed that if an operation is rushed, the time saved at the start may be a misleading savings when the cost of warranty work is put into the cost equation.

What do we mean by "quality"? No organization says its products and services are of average or below average quality. All claim quality as a concern. With the increasing scramble for achieving and maintaining a competitive advantage; corporations, government, and, yes, even educational institutions have embraced a concept, Total Quality Management/Leadership (TQM/L) which demands that the "customer" be the final arbiter of quality. Utilization of Deming's principles plus basic cultural transformation are embodied in a long range effort to deal with the importance of quality in increasing productivity.

· DOING ·

How would we quantify our quality claims? What does our quality do for our sales? If we make a low-end flashlight battery, does the market overlook our quality standard because of our low price? If we make a high-tech cadmium battery, how does our quality give us a competitive edge in spite of its higher price?

Is the money we spend determined by our standard of performance? How might we spend the money differently for the same results? How might we spend less and get more?

How much do we produce? When People Express first got started, it had fewer ground personnel handling greater numbers of passengers than the traditional carriers where personnel were more stratified. People Express had a higher performance standard as a result of a different operational structure. Its productivity was therefore higher.

How do time, money, quality and quantity relate to our performance standards? To productivity?

Productivity and Strategy

Our strategy is dependent upon our productivity. If there is a leading indicator of how well our strategy is working, it is productivity. By concentrating our questioning on ways of raising productivity, we are directing our efforts—and those of everyone involved in operations—in pursuit of our overall strategy.

What are our productivity goals?

How are they related to our strategy?

How are they communicated to everyone in the organization?

Does TQM/L offer our operation a competitive advantage? Survival?

ASKING "JUST RIGHT" BUSINESS QUESTIONS
HOW DO WE GET FEEDBACK

F.D.R.'s Parallel Assignments

Under President Franklin D. Roosevelt, the era of rapid growth in government began. Agency after agency was spawned in an attempt to revolutionize the role of government in influencing the economic fortunes of the country. On top of that, America's entry into World War II required a vast buildup and retooling of the country's natural and industrial resources. The speed and size of the federal government's growth confronted F.D.R. with the danger of being cut off from the grass roots and ground truth. As a politician he prided himself on being in touch with the common man, who also happened to represent his main constituency.

Although confined to a wheelchair and lacking the instant communication networks we take for granted, Roosevelt avoided the Oval Office isolation experienced by many presidents since. One of his favorite methods for getting feedback was to make parallel assignments. F. D. R. would find people in sensitive areas, invite them to the White House, and tell them how much he would appreciate knowing their views on what was going on. Who would turn down the chance to keep the President of the United States informed? However, no individual knew of the others, allowing F.D.R. to compare accounts of what was happening at home and abroad, thereby avoiding the bias of a single version.

Many of the people he chose were outside the normal chains of command of agencies and the military hierarchy. He was never content to rely on one person or one system for vital information. Unable to manage by walking around, he found other ways of getting around.

What are our feedback systems?

What are our formal systems? Our informal systems? How filtered are the systems and who does the filtering?

What is the quality of information from our feedback loops?

• DOING •

How confident are we about the adequacy, timeliness, and amount of feedback we receive?

The Feedback Instinct

Feedback and "noise" need to be separated. Communication theorists define "noise" as the useless static surrounding a message. If there is too much static, the message may get garbled or lost altogether. If we have been a manager in the same organization awhile, trusting our instincts about the adequacy of our feedback is a solid way to start.

What do our instincts tell us about our feedback?

Have the feedback systems been sufficient? Has the information been reliable and, if need be, verifiable? Have there been feedback gaps? Have we felt blindsided?

The Feedback Fix

If we think our feedback pipes are corroded, we should consider whether our problem is in the pipeline or in us—or both. How would we answer questions like these:

> *What would be the ideal feedback system for our organization?*
>
> *What feedback systems have we not used? Underutilized?*

Are there additional contacts we can call upon? Are there systems currently not thought of as feedback loops that could function that way? When Roosevelt came to the White House in 1933, he inherited a feedback system reliant upon the established hierarchy for information. Several years before he had served as Assistant Secretary of the Navy and gained an insider's perspective on how the system worked to keep ideas from getting to the top. As President he sensed that technological and political changes were running at a pace that would overwhelm the feedback systems in place. Example: Developments in aircraft design and their potential for military use were filtered through the political infighting of the Joint Chiefs of Staff. (Generally they were opposed to a separate role for an Air Force because both the

151

ASKING "JUST RIGHT" BUSINESS QUESTIONS

Army and Navy each wanted its own air arm. Roosevelt circumvented the military hierarchy by getting hold of documents before the Joint Chiefs read them. He even approved of recommendations before they could react to them.) He needed—and found—ways of circumventing the feedback systems to get himself in the here–and–now so he would know what was really going on.

When we hear what is going on, are we really listening? Many managers are surer of their listening skills than they have a right to be. We all think we have heard everything said, yet how do we know if we have missed something? Managers subjected to listening skills tests frequently find their scores at 60 to 80 percent. How do we stackup?

How good are our listening skills?

If we say they are excellent, what is our evidence? After all, if we are missing important items, how do we know we are missing them? Do we miss information that others pick up? Are we so preoccupied with "important" matters that other items get by us?

How can we improve our listening skills?

Have we tried *restating* what others have said? Our restatement might show them—and us—gaps in what we heard. Do we *summarize* important findings? A summary can function as a nugget. It can also demonstrate whether we have grasped the essentials.

There is also the matter of what we do with what we get:

What do we do with feedback once we have it?

How is our feedback shared?

In a football game the amount of feedback and the speed with which it comes can be overwhelming. A coach has two options: He can receive all of the information and then *prescribe* what he wants done on the field. In that process he may inadvertently cut off any additional loops for the information to travel through. If the pressure of time and events so dictate, that may be the right decision.

The other option is to *describe* what is happening and make collective decisions, thereby widening the loop by including others. A description invites participation. Approached that way, other perspectives enter the picture—as well as other action options.

> *How inclusive should our feedback loops be? Do we want spectators or participants?*

And Finally—Single Loops or Double Loops

A simple thermostat checks continuously whether the air surrounding it is warmer or cooler than the temperature for which it has been set. Managers monitor their actions against a plan. The thermostat never asks if it is set for the greatest comfort of its surroundings; many managers never ask if the plan was the most appropriate. This is single loop feedback, single loop learning. Humans, and now even "smart" thermostats, have the capability for realizing the value of double loop feedback, double loop learning. The enlightened manager ensures that the second question is asked:

> *Even if this accomplishes what we planned, is this the plan we should have?*
>
> *What may be important to us that we never talk about?*
>
> *Do we squelch feedback which goes beyond what we have asked?*

ASKING "JUST RIGHT" BUSINESS QUESTIONS

HOW ARE WE MANAGING OUR RESOURCE BASE?

All the Organization's Resources Got Wings

The combination of the deep recession and the runaway inflation of the late 1970s and early 1980s forced home the realization of the need for management of all our resources all the time. When resources get scarce, managers ask variations on this theme:

> *What are all of our available resources and how are we managing them?*

What do we list as our available resources? Money? Time? People? Patents? Market Position? Copyrights? Land? How available is each resource to us? What else is there?

Once our definition of resources is clear, we want to know how pervasive the understanding is:

> *How far down the organization is the concern for resources?*

Are the people in the mailroom as concerned for proper management of our resources as is the manager of human management resources and building services? Does the last one out turn off the lights? How much of travel and entertainment budgets go for personal, non-business use? Acts of petty, personal aggrandizement are not costly if judged in isolation, but what do they tell us about related matters:

> *What does unwise use of resources indicate about attitudes toward the organization?*
>
> *What does wise use tell us?*

A Quick Look at Resource Use

Our perspective needs to encompass everything and everyone capable of being a resource:

There is *time*.

> *How creative is our use of time?*

• DOING •

Are our priorities consistent with our use of time? Do we get the most from the time we have? Many years ago insurance companies in Hartford studied productivity on an hourly basis. They discovered that in a nine-to-five day productivity lagged during the last hour. Aside from normal day-end fatigue, the anxiety about being caught in the five o'clock rush diminished effectiveness after 4:00 p.m. The work day was shortened to a 4:30 closing time. Productivity went up, partly because people learned to work a bit faster and were less concerned about the perils of rush hour traffic.

There is *money*.

How well do we manage our money?

Are we as careful in good times as in bad about expenditures? How do we measure the different kinds of returns we get for our investments? What would happen if we managed money differently from the way we do now?

There are *people*.

What are the signs that our human resources are operating at their full potential?

How do we assess the potential of the people we already have? Do we pigeonhole people or encourage them to grow? How do we relate what people are doing for us now to what they might do for us later? How much thought have we given to career paths? To positive motivation? In developing our strategic plan, did we incorporate the training needs of the people who will be carrying out the plan?

There are our *facilities*.

How can we get the most from our existing facilities?

Many private prep schools and colleges rent their dormitories and grounds to outside organizations for special summer schools. Long ago airlines discovered a profitable overnight delivery service could be piggybacked onto existing flights.

There are our *exsiting markets*.

How might existing customers be resources?

ASKING "JUST RIGHT" BUSINESS QUESTIONS

Ordinarily we view an existing client as a market, not as a resource. If our clients and customers have access to information or markets not readily available to us, how can we utilize them?

The Scholastic Publishing Company regularly asks teachers to send students home with descriptions of books for sale. The idea is to get the parents to select the books and send the payment back with the kids. The teachers collect the funds, send them to Scholastic, and later distribute the books for Scholastic. The teachers are both customers of and a resource for Scholastic.

There are *hidden resources.*

How do we discover new uses for discarded resources?

Ordinarily garbage was once thrown away. Many communities, pressed by the need for cheaper fuels for power and a lack of space for garbage, have been converting their garbage into a fuel source. Motion picture companies have discovered their archives as a source of videocassettes for the home video market.

Speaking of E. F. Hutton . . .

E. F. Hutton's financial resource management eventually interested the Department of Justice. Judged strictly in terms of broadening an organization's view of resource use, credit must be accorded to E. F. Hutton for the scheme to receive interest for funds in its possession. Managers at various locations deposited checks for these funds during the early 1980s when interest rates were in double digits. E. F. Hutton thus made money on money not technically its own. Illegalities aside, the scheme managed capital resources to their full potential. Motivated by bonuses and pushed to wring every last benefit from all available resources, many E. F. Hutton managers made a lot of money for E. F. Hutton and themselves. Unfortunately, the Hutton hunt for the *nth* degree of resource management took them from the bottom line to the firing line.

How do we discover new resources?

• DOING •

HOW DO WE ACCOMPLISH DECISION IMPLEMENTATION?

Alphonse and Gaston

The old comic routine involving Alphonse and Gaston trying to decide who goes through the doorway starts:

"You first,"

"No, *you*."

"No, no! *You* first!"

and ends when they collide as each simultaneously attempts to implement the decision.

As we implement our decisions, there will be questions regarding logistics, procedures and consequences. The answers will be easier to find once we have a firm grasp on how our implementation process sets in motion intended and unintended results. If, for example, all major decisions have to be reviewed by higher authorities, what does that imply for dealing with emergencies? If we design elaborate feedback loops, does that slow down processes in need of speed? Alphonse and Gaston never meant to collide—but they did.

How do we implement decisions?

What in our implementation process might be beneficially changed?

Implementation Under the Microscope

If the collision by Alphonse and Gaston had occurred under our management, what would have been our predictable response? Would we have passed it off as a "learning experience"? Would we have tried to figure out who was to blame and find a punishment to fit the crime?

Suppose Alphonse had saved the day by avoiding the collision: Would we have given him a bonus? Would we have stroked him for one minute, or ignored the incident because we expected one of them to figure out what to do?

ASKING "JUST RIGHT" BUSINESS QUESTIONS

Our personal and organizational styles show up in how we assign blame or credit. They can create an atmosphere decisively affecting the implementation process. There are two organizational psychoses whose side effects can inhibit operations; *operational paranoia* and *managerial megalomania*. In paranoia, an unhealthy amount of time is spent digging trenches in anticipation of a hostile invasion: CYA memos are carefully crafted and defensive thinking is cultivated. With megalomania, the symptom is finding fault with others while holding ourselves blameless.

An approximately opposite reaction of lavishing praise for doing the expected and prematurely placing people on pedestals is equally dysfunctional.

The heart of the problem is excess and misdirection. When we carry blame and praise to extremes, focus on surface manifestations instead of fundamentals, we inhibit the implementation process and cripple the *doing* phase.

> *What is our style for recognizing success? Assigning blame?*

Do we try to fix the blame or fix the problem? Do we recognize the people and systems that make the implementation process work the way we want it to? An IBM executive confessed a million-dollar misjudgment to Thomas Watson, Jr. With it he offered his resignation. Watson turned it down because he felt having just paid for a million-dollar "education," he did not want to lose such a valuable employee.

How innovative and creative do we want people to be when implementing our decisions and plans? Are we geniuses who have designed a system to be carried out by idiots? Are we cultivating and transmitting our genius to others?

Two successful baseball managers were Whitey Herzog and Billy Martin. Much of what they knew they learned from the venerable Casey Stengel, for whom they both played. Herzog and Martin designed their successful teams to be aggressive in the use of speed. Herzog allowed his runners to steal when they thought they could pull it off. Martin pulled the strings from the dugout, keeping those decisions for himself. One wanted the implementation process delegated, the other closely regulated. Both won pennants and championships. Both were fired more than once. Who was the better manager? Who had the better implementation system?

Varieties of Ambiguity

Had the Greeks had a god of confusion, its name would have been Ambiguity. When our words and actions take on extra levels of meaning, we may be sowing the seeds of ambiguity. If we go on a belt-tightening campaign to minimize unnecessary expenses, the office furniture we choose and the business trips we take may reinforce or undermine our credibility. If we ask people to take the initiative and punish them for not being successful every time, our actions will be more carefully noted than our words.

What of the model we set for others to follow? If the manager of the supermarket pitches in to bag groceries to relieve clogged checkout lanes, what message is being sent to staff and patrons?

Intended and unintended ambiguities create operational consequences. If some issues are intentionally left open, the implication is that someone else is expected to take charge. When he created People Express, Donald C. Burr spent time in the trenches with the troops, but he was there to see how it was working, not to tell the personnel how to do their jobs.

What about managers who give contradictory messages? The E. F. Hutton managers who got interest on funds not legally in their possession were operating in the open. In fact, they talked to each other. They believed approval of their actions was coming from the top. No one at the top directly told them to break the law, but the rewards given for the extra special utilization of "newly found" resources sent a message encouraging illegal activity.

What is the ambiguity content of our words? Our actions?

What ambiguities are intentional? Unintentional?

Anticipation of the Unknown

In the implementation process of new activities, we try to anticipate what will happen: Building realistic scenarios is one method that can approximate reality.

Scenarios are imagined dry runs of how things will work once they are actually in place. When skilled accountants do scenarios, they can show the dollar consequences in best-case and worst-case projections. If we are trying to foresee how an operation will work, we might want to canvass all of the key people for their assessments. The interplay may educate us all.

These simulations can work like dress rehearsals. They are as close to the real thing as we can afford to make them. Very expensive simulators have been built to train airline pilots and sea captains because, as expensive as the simulation equipment may be, loss of an aircraft or ocean liner would be catastrophic. Most of the time the only practical simulation involves isolating the unknowns and working through what we believe they will be like. Practicing a sales presentation in as realistic a setting as possible can help both inexperienced and experienced people work out the kinks before meeting the customers.

What scenarios and simulations would test our decision- implementation practices?

• DOING •

WHAT IS THE COMMONALITY?

Sherlock Holmes, Asker of Questions

Confronted by a mystery, Sherlock Holmes had the unerring instinct to search out the common element in a pile of disparate pieces. He always found the thread holding together the fabric of the problem. Admittedly he had help: There was Dr. Watson for an additional scientific dimension and a sounding board for Holmes' questions. They were reducible to these three:

What are the similarities?

What are the differences?

What is the key variable?

When problems resist our standard solutions, we can use Sherlock's technique to get at the hidden commonality. It may give us the breakthrough we need.

In searching for *similarities*, look for factors not immediately obvious. In the example of the brewery with the liberal sampling policy, management saw an increase in accidents. What it missed was the alcohol-related nature of the accidents. "What do all of these accidents have in common?" was a question to pursue.

In digging for dissimilarities, try to locate important *differences* in things ordinarily thought to be alike. In industries accustomed to thinking today's labor force is like that of a generation ago, the focus is on similarities, so it might be fruitful to consider the differences. A better-educated, differently motivated labor pool has great potential when its differences with past workers are appreciated. But first they have to be seen.

The *key variable* can uncover both differences and similarities. It is the element that consistently varies when important conditions change. When the accident rate at the generous brewery went up, the suspicious variable was consumption of alcohol. When the accident rate went down with the removal of free beer, the evidence was clear about having located the right variable.

ASKING "JUST RIGHT" BUSINESS QUESTIONS

When "X" changes do "Y" or "Z" vary positively or negatively at the same time? What does "Y" or "Z" have in common with "X"?

Seeing Similarities and Missing Differences

In the early '80s the book publishing segment of the communications industry saw only the similarities between software publishing and book publishing. Top managers reasoned that upscale people were buying personal computers and had a need for software. Hot sellers in books are often in entertainment and self-help, two areas where the early software programs were developed. Software could be packaged, warehoused and sold just like books. Disks could be put in containers with attractive covers, stored alongside books in the warehouses and sold through many of the same distribution channels as books. So into the software sea they all jumped, only to discover they were swimming in red ink up to their corporate necks.

What they missed were the dissimilarities. The differences were fundamental. Only those publishers who saw the similarities *and* the differences came out ahead. Books are usually developed by single authors working with experienced editors. Software required (especially in the early days) a much larger and more expensive development effort, often undertaken by a group. Books rely upon a mature technology, software upon an evolving technology. To keep unit costs down, books have to be run in numbers more sizable than software disks for which there is not the same cost advantage in large runs. Because of the size of the runs, warehouses are organized to take advantage of vertical space (books are stacked). When small runs of software were done, the vertical space above them was charged to them even though it was not used, thereby driving up carrying costs. The disk-using habits of people were not as well established as their reading preferences.

The key variable in software is electronic technology. The development, marketing and use of software is understood best when its electronic nature is comprehended, not when a book publishing system is imposed on it. Had the publishers paid attention to differences they might have organized their manufacturing, marketing and fulfillment efforts in ways more suitable to the emerging software economics.

Selecting Perceptions

Only a Sherlock Holmes—that is, only a fictional character—can avoid the selective perception of reality. We all fall victim to it, especially when championing a plan of action measuring its early returns. There is no therapy for its avoidance, no magic questions to ask guaranteeing its disappearance. There are some signals of its presence to which leaders need to be alert. When looking at similarities and differences with a critical eye and hearing them defended by sentiments like "There's the right way, the wrong way and our way," then it is time to ask "Why?" Anyone getting at why publishers insisted on seeing software as if it were books would have uncovered a case of wishful thinking. They wanted software to be the same as books because to admit the differences would have slowed down their rush to market and forced them into a different way of *doing* things. A line of questioning like:

> *What are the commonalities?*
>
> *How hard have we pursued similarities and differences?*

might have made market entry more profitable.

ASKING "JUST RIGHT" BUSINESS QUESTIONS

HOW DO WE DESIGN USEFUL MEASUREMENT OF RESULTS?

The Three "F's" for Measuring Results

We can help clarify our measurement results by applying three criteria: *fundamentals, frequency,* and *format.* Each is dealt with separately here only for the purposes of analysis. Interweaving them with our measurement concerns is a key management task.

Fundamentals in an organization are like the vital signs in an organism. We have to determine the rates of metabolism and heartbeat of what we are doing, how the respiratory and digestive systems are working and so on. When putting the stethoscope to the organization, what are we listening for and where are we listening for it?

> *What is the single most important indicator of how we are doing? How can it be isolated?*
>
> *What is the next most important indicator? The next after that?*

We are looking for essentials.

If we are tracking market response to the introduction of a new product, what will tell us about essentials? The number of buyers? Their identity? What kinds of variables should be watched? In air fare wars, is it passenger occupancy rates, cost per mile or some combinations?

We need to identify patterns of behavior such as response to variety, geographic variations, price sensitivity, premiums, seasonality, or that essential indicator telling us something critical about what is going on in our market.

Everyone has received the stamp sheets from Publishers Clearing House. Monthly it sends discount subscription offers to millions of prospective subscribers. Results are measured by analyzing the maximum and minimum number of stamps to use in an offering, which magazines perform best, what offers work most successfully, the placement of stamps on the sheet, the role of sweepstakes, payment and nonpayment patterns, preferences by age and sex, and so forth. Given the millions of letters sent and the millions of subscriptions received, Publishers Clearing House needs feedback tailored to the key variables of magazine subscription buyers. Changes in purchasing habits are especially important: Subscription offers for shorter durations have become preferred over longer ones. There are dollar limits to any offering. In order to grow, PCH has experimented with selling magazine-related products, such as audiocassettes and books. The way it measures results determines the new product directions it is willing to take.

Frequency needs to be considered from many angles: The more often we ask for results to be shown to us, the more work we are creating in their preparation. In addition, we may run the risk of seeing artificial trends.

If we have a field sales force, our uneasiness in being isolated from the action can lead us to ask for more reports than is good for us to have or for the salespeople to write: Do we want them writing reports or making sales calls? Do we want them polishing their writing skills or practicing their selling skills?

> *How much time should there be between reports?*
>
> *What kind of burdens and distractions will reports impose?*
>
> *What happens when there are too many reports too much of the time?*
>
> *What do we do with the reports we say we need?*

Format can determine how accessible a report is. How much attention are we paying to making a form follow its function?

> *How do we ensure verbal and visual clarity?*

By paying close attention to our audience, we can adjust the format to their need to know.

> *What can be left out without damaging the essential content?*
>
> *How can we summarize results?*
>
> *What form should that summary take?*

ASKING "JUST RIGHT" BUSINESS QUESTIONS

A short paragraph and a two-dimensional chart can condense a half-dozen pages into a single sheet. During his years as Governor of California and in his presidency, Ronald Reagan insisted on one-page summaries of all major issues. Some chalked it up to an avoidance of dealing with facts. Others saw it as the only way a chief executive could deal with so many complex issues.

Here–and–Now Results Compared to Yesterday's Concerns

Questions about measuring results in the *doing* phase are descendants from our earlier concerns in *seeing*. Like everything else within our organization, the goals and objectives that have taken us to where we are now are subject to change. Results need to trigger the automatic review of goals and objectives. Time will have passed between the time we formed plans and when we put them into play. So:

> *What do current results tell us about our goals and objectives?*

Do we need to adjust or overhaul them? Are they demonstrating our vision then about what would happen now—or our myopia? When Eastern Airlines went to the considerable expense of modernizing its aircraft, its goal was a lower fuel cost per passenger mile. As new equipment came on line, the cost picture improved. Conditions had changed because of the breakup of OPEC solidarity and the inroads made by discount carriers. Fuel costs were a lesser issue by the time Eastern neared completion of its upgrading program. How should Eastern have modified its monitoring of results?

• DOING •
HOW EFFECTIVE AND EFFICIENT IS OUR OPERATION?

The "Effectancy" Goal

Never at rest, our language constantly absorbs new words. Those catching on describe something captivating our imaginations, enabling us to articulate an idea better. Our entry is "effectancy." Its creator is David Carpenter, Chairman and CEO of TransAmerica/Occidental Life Insurance Company. He wanted to weld together the concepts of being *effective* and *efficient* so he coined "effectancy." TransAmerica/Occidental Life actively uses it as a measure of how effective and efficient it is in its operations.

When we accomplish what we set out to do, we are *effective*. But if in doing it we create consequences we did not want, then we are *inefficient* even though we have been effective. If we are running an airline and our objective is to fill every plane, we may overbook. If the overbooking requires us to pay off too many passengers, our effectiveness leads to inefficiency.

The flip side is when efficiency gets in the way of effectiveness. If those preparing reports for us spend too much time making them look professional, they achieve efficiency but make us pay the price in effectiveness.

What are we doing to be more effective?

What does effectiveness do to efficiency?

How do we become more efficient?

What do our efficiency needs do to our effectiveness?

The relationship between the effective and the efficient should be on our minds every time we talk about either. Consider the idea in the pursuit of objectives:

How effectively are we reaching our objectives?

How efficiently are we reaching our objectives?

With a constant supply of cheap, non-union labor, the Egyptian pharaohs reached their objectives of ever bigger pyramids.

ASKING "JUST RIGHT" BUSINESS QUESTIONS

Their costs were relatively low: food for the workers, salaries for their managers and soldiers. Efficiency was helped by materials being cheap in those days. Suppose, however, Moses had been a labor leader instead of a promised–land locator. If he had successfully unionized his people, the pharaoh would have had to settle for a smaller pyramid because of skyrocketing labor costs. Otherwise the achievement of his big-pyramid objectives would have been inefficient.

A changeover to robotics makes sense when it strikes the best balance between the effective and the efficient. High labor costs and concerns for quality control may lead to a switch to automation technology on an assembly line where effectiveness counts. But the start-up costs, maintenance, and danger of robot obsolescence can raise efficiency issues. Questions of this nature are what General Motors is wrestling with at its Saturn assembly plant.

The Pandora's Box Perplex

We know what happened when Pandora's box was opened: More came out than anticipated and the problem was compounded when she could not get the lid back on. As we strive to be more effective and efficient, we need to remind ourselves that we do not always know until afterward whether we have a Pandora's Box in our midst.

How do we project the efficiency consequences of effectiveness actions?

Estimates keep growing as to the costs of making a personal sales visit. The costs of salary, travel, materials and maintenance expenses can grow faster than sales volume. Since direct selling is the most efficient way to sell many things, its cost effectiveness has to be watched. National sales managers analyze how many dollars a field representative has to generate to be cost effective enough to be kept in the field. Often they consider alternatives—like direct mail and telemarketing—to determine whether there are more effective and efficient sales channels.

How do we test more effective alternatives?

The French Fries Course at Hamburger University

If ever there was a model for combining the effective with the efficient, it is at Hamburger University. The school was founded by the McDonald's Corporation to train managers in the art and craft of running a McDonald's hamburger franchise.

McDonald's had a vision of how a fast food operation can be effective, efficient and highly profitable. Obviously the food has to be prepared—but not at the cost of appearance and taste. If families are to be induced to have a meal at a McDonald's, fastidious mothers and suspicious fathers should be confident of bringing their kids into a squeaky-clean place. No bedraggled burgers, no soggy fries, and plenty of perceived value at rock-bottom prices.

To keep operational costs low, McDonald's has found a way to employ people at the low end of the labor skills spectrum, like teenagers and high school graduates just beginning to learn about working, or retired senior citizens who will accept part-time, no fringe, minimum wage jobs.

To make its labor force an effective and efficient means of meeting competitive objectives, McDonald's trains its own managers and designs its own equipment. There is a McDonald's approach to French Fries. The end result is a carton of fries brimming over. It is achieved through the design of a box slightly smaller than the number of fries it holds, thereby ensuring the full look. The scoop used to fill the carton was designed to hold the right number of fries on the first scoop. The scooping motion needed to bring fries, carton and scooper together is prescribed. After all, speed is at the heart of a fast food operation, so motion is a subject of interest to management. Future managers learn how it is all done at Hamburger University. Their job is to train others in the art of preparing and distributing food fast. If there were ratings for efficiency, McDonald's establishments would rank at the top.

ASKING "JUST RIGHT" BUSINESS QUESTIONS
WHAT ARE THE CHANGE INDICATORS?

Operational Snapshots

We are at the end of our question units—but not at the end of our questioning. This is the time for many of the questions to be recycled in the light of all the questions we have been asking. "Just right" questions are hitched together by this consideration:

What is happening inside and outside our organization since we started the questioning process?

As we ask and answer questions, a process of change may have taken place, requiring recent insights to be refined. Constant change is the underlying reality of management, so:

Will we manage change or will change manage us?

To get a handle on change, we take operational snapshots, still photos of the dynamic processes critical to the health and future of our enterprise. Those snapshots can be financial reports, progress updates, formal projections, outside consultants' studies, or whatever helps us understand how we are doing and what we ought to be doing. As with any photograph or blueprint, we need to be aware of the *perspectives* of the reporters, the *timeliness* of the report, the *direction* it is heading in, and its true *intent:*

Begin with the *timeliness* of an operational picture.

How current is our snapshot?

Because we are looking at something from the past, such as a projection based on past data, there is an aging factor. In the unit on results measurement, we cautioned about how long information gathering and actual transmission can take. Has anything new occurred to make a recent operational snapshot outdated?

What is our angle of vision?

The *perspective* of the picture taker can determine the picture's effect on the viewer. The *perspective* of a number–cruncher may be to see everything in terms of numbers, ignoring important qualitative aspects. The inventory manager may see only objects filling spaces at a certain cost per foot.

> *Does the focus of our attention cover all the critical areas?*

We should always press for a forward-looking *direction*, using the past to explain the present, not justify it. Operational snapshots require interpretation:

> *What is the nature of our forward progress?*

Are we fumbling forward? Are we being carried by the market or are we leading the market?

> *What do our operational snapshots tell us about where we are headed? How are we getting there?*

What about *intentions*? Have our operational snapshots become ritualized? Are they fresh and vital? Do the operational snapshots aim to justify, mystify or clarify?

> *How posed are our operational snapshots?*
>
> *How candid?*
>
> *How crucial are our operational snapshots to what we do?*

Should they not be vital enough, or if they obscure what we need to know, then it is time to rethink the way operational snapshots are prepared.

> *How can we revitalize our operational snapshots?*

Looking for Change Indicators

The best reasons for making changes are new conditions and new opportunities. Detecting them early and doing something about them can hone a competitive edge.

When looking for change indicators, we need to figure out what potential there is for us:

> *What change indicators should we watch closely?*
>
> *If we see them, what should we do?*

The indicators vary with industries and instincts. The indicators depend on the intelligence we can get, our freedom of action, and the courage of our convictions. They may be statistics about demographics, legal trends, cultural developments, technological breakthroughs. They may be involved with how the planet itself is evolving or the price of coffee beans in Columbia. We never get very far without some information on which we can base some conclusions:

> *What ripple effect will come from the indicators we follow?*

Rather than be greeted with gratitude, change is more likely to be resisted with vigor. Talk about change can be preferred to making changes. Managing change is our final test.

> *How should what we have been "doing" be changed by what we have been "seeing"?*

> *How do we identify the need to change?*

> *How will we manage change?*

EPILOGUE

The Road To Implementation

WHAT DO WE DO WITH OUR ANSWERS

This Question's for You!

Red Scott, as the CEO of Intermark, a holding company in southern California, is an astute question-asker. Whenever he contemplates acquiring a company, he asks what is involved in getting from where he is to where it is. If the trip takes more than two hours by air, it is a negative factor because he believes his success depends on keeping in touch with the companies he owns.

Occasionally Scott gives seminars on his management style to groups of executives. Their content has differed but the way they begin and end is constant. At the start he announces that two questions will be asked at the end of the session. The first will be:

What have you learned here that you can take back to your job?

because he likes his audiences to be thinking ahead during the seminar. That keeps the focus on why they came.

The second question is divulged at the end when Scott canvasses his audience to see what different people have learned and can take back to their jobs.

Then he asks the question he considers to be equally important as what people have learned:

How will you implement what you say you have learned?

The world is awash in good ideas. Unless ways are found to implement them, those ideas will be little more than academic exercises. No matter where our answers come from—from asking questions or hiring consultants or reading books—their worth is realized when they are put into practice. Now that you have come

ASKING "JUST RIGHT" BUSINESS QUESTIONS

to the end of a book about asking "just right" questions, you have arrived at the beginning of the implementation process.

Questions in the Path of Progress

Fear of change and *concern for distraction* are two common barriers to implementing new answers. Fear of change is an emotionally–based response. There is, after all, comfort in pre-dictable routines. Should a new piece of automated office equipment or a new idea about markets be introduced, the resistance encountered may be based on having to do things differently rather than on any drawbacks of the idea or the device. The reasons people give for resisting often mask the true roots of resistance.

> *What underlying causes might there be for resistance to new answers?*
>
> *How do we deal with irrationally based obstacles?*

A more thoughtful, rational obstacle is a genuine concern for distraction. When we ask people to do old things in a new way, or to do something different, how will that affect continuing activities?

> *What demands will our new ideas make on our organizations?*

Resistance to new answers can be in an organization's wider interests. The case can be made for introducing change slowly—or not at all—so that the heritage of the past and the promise of the future are not wrecked by the opportunities of the present.

> *What is our plan for introducing new answers?*
>
> *What kinds of resistance might we meet?*

The National Geographic Society, publishers of *National Geographic* and sponsor of numerous television specials, is a nonprofit organization. Any new idea, no matter how beneficial it could be, is measured against any danger the idea might pose to the organization's tax–exempt status. The organization is more than self-sufficient, it has made highly satisfactory profits on its activities over the years—all within the legal conditions of what not-for-profit organizations are permitted. All new ideas about

• EPILOGUE •

growth, markets, products and operations are viewed through the prism of its tax status. It is a rational question process about consequences: There are no benefits large enough to offset the loss of that advantage.

Years ago the *Reader's Digest* was a monthly magazine of condensed articles and books. The magazine's profits came strictly from its subscription base. It carried no advertisements, a state unimaginable now. It was popular, growing and profitable. Within the *Digest's* organization were those champing at the bit to carry advertisements. Although the case was made for the benefits of opening the magazine to advertising, there was stiff resistance: How would readers react? Would advertisers influence policy? How would the *Digest* change?

At first the magazine carried a few ads, closely monitoring any adverse reaction from readers. Beginning with those early days of going commercial, the *Digest* entered a path to rapid and profitable growth. Carrying ads opened up a vision of its subscription base as customers for more than condensations. Today the Reader's Digest Association is profitably engaged in all aspects of exploiting its customer base as a book and magazine publisher.

ASKING "JUST RIGHT" BUSINESS QUESTIONS
WHO WILL CHAMPION THE CAUSE?

Stepping In

The *entrepreneur* is fundamental to free market systems. Jobs and Wozniak founded Apple Computer around their idea of a home market for the personal computer. Their successor, John Sculley, took over the entrepreneurial problems inherent in maturing markets.

When the questions we ask deal with markets, the answers we get will require an entrepreneurial approach to implementation. They will be market-driven:

> *What will it take to implement new ideas in our markets?*

The idea of an "intrapreneur" is being stimulated by the needs of change within organizations. Many of our entrepreneurial models are folk heroes: The Ben Franklins and Thomas Edisons are used as examples of people who could take an idea and run with it. But what of those whose ideas first require changes within? There are heroes and heroines, but they are less well known: There were Thomas Watson, Sr., at IBM. Alfred Sloan at General Motors, and Joan Ganz Cooney at the Children's Television Workshop. Each had to first implement ideas within his/her organization before they could go outside with them. They needed to build the internal structure before they could move to external markets. Therefore they are internal champions, intrapreneurs.

> *How do we implement ideas within our own organization?*

> *What parts of our organization will be touched by our implementation process?*

Stepping Out

We need to keep the implementation process boiling. The kinds of questions supporting the cause are of the here-and-now, action-oriented variety:

> *Who will be responsible?*

• EPILOGUE •

If there is a committee, look to the chair of that committee to take responsibility for energizing the committee.

What is needed to make it happen?

We look for concrete steps, not just talk.

The question we have seen successfully used is the "just right" question to close with:

What is the next step?

ASKING "JUST RIGHT" BUSINESS QUESTIONS

ADDITIONAL READING SUGGESTIONS

HOW SHOULD WE BE READING?

Let the Strategy Fit the Reading

There is never enough time to read everything available to stay professionally sharp. There are tempting shortcuts like digest of articles and audiocassette boil-downs of top-selling books. Most of their value is in the illusions they create—not in the benefits they bring.

To stay on top of the mountain of reading material, a professional manager has to develop a reading strategy. If the strategy mixes the contemporary and classic, that manager will develop a breadth of understanding both to develop "just right" questions and to utilize "just right" answers.

Used in tandem, the contemporary current magazine and newspapers and classic books and journals feed each other and expand each other's applications to our current needs.

We recommend four tactics:

1. *Rotate the sources.* If the magazines and newspapers we read are always the same, we run the risk of cutting off new points of view. If we change the news providers, we vary the viewpoints. If you subscribe to *Time*, try *Newsweek* for a while. If you travel, read the local newspapers—especially their editorial pages—to get a feel for regional differences.

2. *Know the house rules.* Most newspaper stories and magazine articles are the products of teamwork and house rules. There are few star reporters whose words are printed exactly the way they were submitted. If you look closely, for example, at the styles of *Time, Forbes, Newsweek, U.S. News and World Report* and *The Economist,* you will see distinctive differences in

• ADDITIONAL READING SUGGESTIONS •

perspective and policy. The policies influence what is said and not said, what is covered and what is ignored. Keep in mind that magazines and newspapers are products aimed at particular audiences.

3. *Read book reviews.* The major newspapers and magazines regularly carry reviews of the latest books of which managers should be aware. The *New York Times Book Review* and the *New York Review of Books* are two comprehensive and quality publications devoted entirely to book reviewing. The *Times* carries the *Book Review* as a regular supplement to its Sunday edition, but it is available separately, as is the *New York Review of Books*. Both publications are usually available in bookstores and libraries.

Magazines and journals specializing in business and management concerns generally confine their reviews to books on those subjects. Magazines like *Time, Newsweek, The Economist, Business Week* and *Fortune,* newspapers like the *Wall Street Journal,* and professional journals like *Harvard Business Review* and *Sloan Management Review* specialize in reviewing books likely to be of interest to executives.

A few of the major newspapers have extensive business sections carrying articles of current interest to managers using a question-asking style. The *New York Times,* the *Los Angeles Times,* and the *Washington Post* are among the best choices.

4. *Allow time for books and articles.* Broadly speaking, newspaper and magazine articles are aimed at topical subjects—what is happening right now—whereas books and journals hope to explore in depth subjects of lasting interest—what will continue to happen. To read either at the expense of the other is to cut off a major source of thoughtful questions. Time for both is essential.

WHAT BOOKS AND ARTICLES MIGHT STIMULATE "JUST RIGHT" QUESTIONS?

List Readers Should Beware of List Makers

Our selection criteria for the lists that follow are manageability and appropriateness. The list is not so long as to be overwhelming. The selections are aimed at sharpening the asking and implementing of questions. Some of the pieces are now regarded as classics, others may become so.

We selected books by authors whose approach is not to tell readers what to do but, rather, what to think about. They are the kinds of authors who can stimulate questions you can use. We chose articles particularly on target for one or more of the three questions types—*seeing*, *aiming* or *doing*—and in journals available in most libraries.

Some Great Books by Some Great Authors

Peter Drucker, *Management: Tasks—Responsibilities—Practices* (Harper and Row, 1974). Drucker is the most influential thinker about management problems and practices. This is the book which established management as a science and Drucker as its major spokesperson. It is a long book meant to be read over time, not at a sitting. His style makes his message easy to comprehend. There are many other books by Drucker as well as periodic articles on management on the editorial page of the *Wall Street Journal,* to which he is a regular contributor.

Theodore Levitt, *The Marketing Mode: Pathways to Corporate Growth* (McGraw-Hill, 1969). A Harvard professor, Levitt was also the Editor of the *Harvard Business Review.* He has a light touch and the ability to make a reader relate to wider issues. Levitt sees an organization in terms of the markets it serves and how those markets ought to affect planning, organizing and operating—*aiming* and *doing.*

Chester I. Barnard, *The Functions of the Executive* (Harvard University Press, 1974). First published in 1938, this book has

• ADDITIONAL READING SUGGESTIONS •

been through several editions and continues to pass the test of time. Barnard was the President of New Jersey Bell. Introspective about how he as an executive should function, he put his thoughts down in a style reminiscent of Aristotle. It is not easy reading but it is highly stimulative of *seeing* and *aiming* questions.

Harold D. Stolovitch and Erica J. Keeps (Ed.) *Handbook of Human Performances Technology: A Comprehensive Guide for Analyzing and Solving Performance Problems in Organizations* (Jossey–Bass, 1992). In the "Afterword" by Robert Mager, it is noted, "If you were to read this entire volume at a single sitting, it would be easy to feel overwhelmed by the sheer magnitude...etc." If one reads selected sections, the "just right" questions flow out of this modern classic.

Rensis Likert and Jan Gibson Likert, *New Ways of Managing Conflict* (McGraw-Hill, 1976). It looks and reads like a textbook and is used in many universities and executive programs. The analyses of why conflicts occur and what might be done to manage them will bring out many issues about one's leadership style as well as *doing* questions. The self-revealing personality inventories can bring a deeper understanding of ourselves and the people we manage.

Will and Ariel Durant, *The Lessons of History* (Simon and Schuster, 1968). A distillation of their ten-volume, *The Story of Civilization,* this book helps put the future into perspective. Its best application would be in raising *seeing* kinds of questions. A timeless classic.

Charles H. Kepner and Benjamin B. Tregoe, *The New Rational Manager* (Princeton Research Press, 1981). The authors left the Rand Corporation in the 1950s to found an organization dedicated to a rational approach to decision-making. They found that effective managers tend to ask the same kinds of questions. They built a rational model of the kinds of questions and activities associated with above-average problem solving and decision making. (An earlier version was *The Rational Manager,*

ASKING "JUST RIGHT" BUSINESS QUESTIONS

first published in 1965 and then issued as a second edition in 1976 by Kepner-Tregoe, Inc.)

William Porter, *The Competitive Advantage* (Free Press, 1985). For developing *seeing*, *aiming* and *doing* questions, this book will turn out to be a comprehensive guide. Don't let its size scare you away: It reads easily and delivers on what its title promises. (An earlier William Porter book, *The Competitive Strategy* (Free Press, 1980), sets the stage for strategic questions in the broadest contexts—economics, behavioral science, organizational theory, and so on—and helped establish Porter as a strategic guru.) A later book, *The Competitive Advantage of Nations,* 1990, broadens this perspective to global considerations.

Peter Senge, *The Fifth Discipline* (Doubleday/Currency, 1990). This is subtitled, "The Art and Practice of the Learning Organization." If you don't ask questions you have a "learning disability." This book has gained classic status. It will stimulate a million questions about your organization.

Gareth Morgan, *Imaginization: the Art of Creative Management* (Sage, 1993). This delightful, creative approach to analyzing your organization and *seeing*, *aiming* and *doing* in a more imaginative organization, opens a new age.

Ralph D. Stacey, *Managing the Unknowable* (Jossey–Bass, 1992). This highly provocative book can lead you to questions of discovery in your day-to-day *doing*. Recognizing that the future is truly unknowable, questions about the apparently chaotic present may help you to leverage small chance changes into major strategically competitive successes.

And finally, two more suggestions for staying current and for asking your own "just right" questions.

Information appears in professional journals at least one year, and sometimes two years, before it is published in book form. (Although this time may be shrinking due to changes in printing technology, i.e. desk top publishing, etc.) Developing the habit of visiting a full service library every few months and searching the professional journals in your area of interest can be of immense

• ADDITIONAL READING SUGGESTIONS •

value. If you wish to explore in-depth on a particular topic, talk with the Research Librarian.

The other (and last) suggestion is, *The Manager's Bookshelf: A Mosaic of Contemporary Views*. (3rd Edition, Harper Collins, 1993). Edited by Jon Pierce and John Newstrom. These editions contain a collage of "...many aspects of organizational management from the perspective of a diverse group of management writers..." It includes both summaries from books and articles from professional journals The editors suggest that "this collage can provide you with useful insights, stimulate your thinking and spark some dialogue with your colleagues about the management of today's organizations." They are correct.

Index

A

ABC, 84, 140, 141, 142, 150
Aiming
 audiences and, 98
 business environment and, 1
 business environment and, 90
 complexity levels and, 71
 mission statement and, 64
 objectives and, 103
 organizing principles and, 68
 resources and, 81
 segments and, 75
 strategic options and, 106
 trends watching and, 84
Air France, 75, 76, 77
Airline industry, 20, 94
Alternatives
 action and, 54
 anxiety and, 53
 contingencies and, 52
 effectiveness of, 168
 fresh ideas and, 107
Ambiguity, varieties of, 159
Analogies, thinking patterns and, 48, 49
Anxiety, alternatives and, 53
Apple Computer, 1, 2, 4, 8, 23, 87, 106, 108, 124, 176
Assumptions
 directions and, 33
 facts and, 35
 goals and, 46
 intuitive thinking and, 34
AT&T, 24, 25, 46, 48, 49, 66
Audiences
 defining, 98
 external and internal, 99
 messages and, 72
 readiness levels and, 100, 101
 strategic plan and, 74
Augmentations, innovation and, 26

Authority
 clarifying structure and, 128
 establishing responsibility and, 127
Auto Industry, 1, 3, 4
Avery, Sewell, 33, 48
Avoidance behavior, here-and-now and, 130
Avon Industries, 26

B

Baker International, 52, 53, 69, 78
Baker Oil Tool, 78
Baker-Hughes, 52
Ballantine Books, 40
Banana Republic, 108
Banking, inflation and, 81
Barnard, Chester I., 180
Bay of Pigs, invasion, 55
Bellwether states, 82
Book warehousing, economics of, 162
Bottlenecks, critical paths and, 115
Breweries, 133
Burr, Donald C., 159
Business environment
 governmental policies and, 92
 influencing factors and, 90
 standardization and, 91

C

Career changes, 49
CBS, 31, 40, 54, 84, 140
Change
 business environment and, 90
 control and, 135
 indicators of, 170, 171
 reality and, 132

strategy or tactics, 108
tactics and, 112
transformation vs., 25
Characteristics, organizational culture and, 24
China, 52, 75
Chrysler, 3,4,123,124,143
CNN, 84
Coca-Cola, 44, 45, 46, 79, 108, 112, 113, 114, 122, 135
Code, communication and, 136,138
Commitment
alignment of, 141
securing of, 140
style of, 142
Commonality, definition of, 161
Communications industry, publishing, 162
Communications
objectives and, 136
style and, 137
Competition
comparing strategy and, 63
conditions affecting, 87
financial factors and, 93
internal and external, 96
productivity and, 25
strategy and, 60
Competitive Advantage of Nations (Porter, W.), 182
Competitive Strategy, The (Porter, W.), 182
Conceptualization, 8
Concorde, 75, 76
Constitution, 138
Continental Airlines, 60
Contingencies, 53, 106, 107
Controls, 122, 123, 124, 125, 137
Corp Think, 49
Corporate name, 23
Critical path thinking, 116
Cultural heritage, 6
Cultural reactions, 87

D

Decisions
implementation of, 157
personality in, 121
Deming, W. Edward, 147, 148
Deregulation, 20, 24, 60, 92, 129, 132
Disappointing Search for Excellence, (Carroll, D.), 90
Discover card, 80, 113, 114
Doing
as phases of an idea, 9, 10
change indicators and, 170
commitment and, 141
communications and, 133, 136
control and, 122
decisions and, 158
efficiency and, 167
feedback and, 150
management styles and, 118
power integration and, 126
productivity and, 147
resource management and, 154
results measurement and, 164
role expectations and, 144
tactics of, 112
Doubleday, 103, 115, 116, 117, 182
Dow Jones, 1
Drucker, Peter F., 7, 124, 180
Durant, Will and Ariel, 181

E

Eastern Airlines, 166
Eastman Kodak, 21
Efficiency and effectiveness, 167, 168, 169
Emergencies, 53, 157
Energy Business, 23
Energy Resources, 82
Entrepreneur, 176
Exxon, 23, 24, 30, 31, 45, 69

F

Facilities, 116, 155
Farming, 32
Fawcett Books, 40, 41
Feedback, 136, 137, 150, 151, 152, 153
Fifth Discipline, The (Senge, P.), 182
Fleming, Ted Jr., 97
Fleming Packaging, 97
Fleming, Theodore, 96
Ford, Henry, 34, 118
Ford Motor Company, 148
Forecasting, 37, 38
Format, 164, 165
Format Wars, 90
Fox TV, 84
Frequency, 164, 165
Frontier Airlines, 65
Fuller Brush Man, 26
Functions of the Executive, The (Barnard, C.), 180
Fundamentals, 164
Fundamentals, market, 135
Future, 36, 37, 38, 54, 130

G

Gatekeepers, 99
Geneen, Harold, 124, 131, 142
General Motors, 3
Gillette, 21
Globalized Marketplace, 92
GM, 4, 9, 10, 11, 144, 145, 146
GM Saturn, 127
Goals, 44, 45, 46, 47
Goals, productivity, 149
Government, policy changes, 90
Government, role of, 92, 150
Group think, 55, 56

H

Hamburger University, 169

Hammurabi's Code, 136, 138
Handbook of Human Performances Technology:, (Stolovich & Keeps), 181
HBO (Home Box Office), 28
Here-and-Now Orientation, 130, 132
Herzog, Whitey, 158
Hutton, E. F., 156, 159

I

Iacocca, Lee, 4, 123, 124, 142, 143,
IBM, 2, 28, 29
    Central Attraction, 79
    Organizing Principle, 68, 70
    Sales Expansion, 94
    Strategic Options, 106, 107
    Strategy, 60, 61, 63
    Structure, 62
Ideas
    fresh, 107
    implementation of, 176
    new, 174
    successful, 8
    unique, 26
Identity, 23
Imaginization: the Art of Creative Management (Morgan, G.), 182
In Search of Excellence, 5, 90
Innovation, 28
Innovation means, 26
Intermark, 173
Intrapreneur, 176
Intuition, 34, 35
ITT, 124, 131, 142

J

Japanese, 4, 8, 116
    automakers, 3
    culture, 6
    productivity, 147
    Quality Circles, 137

Jobs, Steven, 2, 8, 106, 176

K

KCET, 9
Kennedy, John F., 55
Kissinger, Henry, 57

L

Label, mfg., 96
Lessons of History, The
   (Durant, W. & A.), 181
Levitt, Theodore, 20, 132, 180
Likert, Rensis and Jan Gibson, 181
Lockheed Corp., 88, 89, 118, 119

M

McDonald's Corporation, 169
Mager, Robert F., 181
Magnetic Tape, technology, 48
Management
   audiences and, 99
   by objectives (MBO), 44
   communications and, 137
   contingency planning and, 108,
   control systems of, 122, 124
   Information Services (MIS), 123
   objectives evaluation by, 103, 104, 105
   power integration and, 126, 129
   productivity and, 147
   readiness levels and, 101
   resource use and, 154
   styles of, 118, 119, 121
   tactics and, 112
Management: Tasks-Responsibilities- Practice
   (Drucker, P.), 180
Manager's Bookshelf:,The, 183
Managing the Unknowable
   (Stacey, R.), 182
Market Analysis, 124

Marketing
   controls and, 124
   goals and, 46
   mindsets and, 51
   objectives and, 66
   summary language and, 73
Marketing Mode: Pathways to Corporate Growth (Levitt, T.), 180
Markets
   audiences and, 98
   changes and, 135
   entrepreneurs, intrapreneurs and, 176
   mission statement and, 64
   segments of, 75
   strategic options and, 106
   strategy and, 60
   trends and, 84
Martin, Billy, 158
Matsushita Electric, 91
MBO (Managing by Objectives), 44
MEGO Scale, 71
Mercedes-Benz, 51, 144, 146, 148
Mexican Government, 81
MIS (Management Information Systems), 123
Mission statements, 64, 68
Montgomery Ward, 33, 48
Morgan, Gareth, 182
Morgan, J. P., 87

N

NASA, 26, 81, 82
National Geographic, 174
National Geographic Society, 174
NBC, 84, 85, 98, 140
Neiman-Marcus, 21, 22
New Rational Manager, The
   (Kepner & Tregoe), 181
New Ways of Managing Conflict
   (Likert & Likert), 181
New York Mets, 101, 103, 104

Nixon, Richard M., 55
Normandy invasion, 126

O

Objectives
  commitment to, 142
  communication of, 136, 138, 139
  content and, 65, 66
  evaluation, 103, 104
  feedback and, 137
  goals and, 44
  identity and, 23
Oil business, 23, 39
Operational (Doing), 9, 10
Operational change, 170, 171
Organizational Culture, 24, 25
Organizational
  goals, 61
  psychoses, 158
  response, 53
  structure, 119, 120
  structure and strategy, 62
  values, 24
Organizing Principle, 68, 69, 70, 71

P

Packaging industry, 97
Panasonic, 91
People as resource, 147, 155
People Express, 60-66, 69, 70-75, 101, 128, 129, 132, 149, 159
Pepsi-Cola, 44, 112
Performance evaluation, 103, 104, 105
Performance payoffs, 145
Performance standards, 148
Period of expansion, 82
Personality, conflicts and, 134
Personality, management styles and, 120, 121, 137
PERT, 115
Phases, 8, 10, 14

Phillips, 91
Polaroid, 68
Porter, William, 182
Potter, Harley, 96
Power, integration of, 126, 127, 128, 129
Productivity, 25, 129, 155
  achievement of, 147, 149
Program for Evaluation and Review Technique (PERT), 115
Public broadcasting stations, 3, 9
Publishers Clearing House, 164, 165
Publishing industry, 27, 40, 48, 90, 115, 162

Q

Quality, 4, 145, 147, 148, 149, 150, 168, 179
Quality circles, 132, 137
Question-asking techniques, 12
Questions, 6, 8, 10, 12, 13, 15, 16, 161, 166, 174
Questions, list of, 17

R

Radio, 77
Railroad, industry of, 20, 24, 92, 132
Random House, 40
Rational Manager, The (Kepner & Tregoe), 181
RCA, 85, 91
Readiness levels, 100, 101
Reagan, administration of, 166
Reagan, Ronald, 92
Regents Air, 75, 76
Regulation, government, 48, 92
Reports, result measurement, 165
Resources, 42, 46, 96
  evaluation of, 30, 31, 32

management of, 154, 155, 156
  origin of, 81
Results, measurement of, 164, 165, 166
Retail, strategy and, 113, 114
Risk
  analysis of, 41
  assumption of, 35
  profiles of, 40
Risk Think, 42
Rockefeller, John D., 23, 39, 118
Role
  anticipation of, 78
  expectations of, 144
  government and, 150
  intuition and, 34
  managerial expertise and, 90
  view of, 142
Roles, people, 145
Roosevelt, Franklin D., 150, 151, 152
Ryan, Nolan, 102

S

Safety, measures of, 133
Scholastic Publishing Co., 156
Scott, Red, 173
Sculley, John, 2, 106, 107, 124, 176
Sears, 33, 45, 69, 80, 109, 113, 114
Seaver, Tom, 102
Seeing
  alternatives and, 52
  assumptions and, 33
  business objectives and, 20
  future and, 36
  goal development and, 44
  innovation and, 26
  resources and, 30
  risk taking and, 40
  starting over and, 55
  thinking patterns and, 48
Senge, Peter, 182
Sony, 30, 91
Sports, spectator, 98

Stacey, Ralph D., 182
Standard Oil, 23, 24, 30, 118
Steinbrenner, George, 99
Stengel, Casey, 101, 158
Stolovitch, Harold D., 181
Strategic Objectives, 10
Strategic Options, 106, 107
Strategic Plan
  complexity level and, 71
  evaluation of, 103
  goals of, 44
Strategic planning, change of objectives and, 105
Strategic Processes, 9
Strategizing, 10
Strategy
  altered environment and, 3
  articulation of, 61
  change and, 108
  competitors and, 63
  grand plan and, 60
  options and, 108
  pricing and, 21
  productivity and, 149
  structure and, 62
  tactical change and, 114
SWOT, 41, 65

T

Tactics
  change of, 113, 114
  changes to, 107, 108
  support of strategy and, 112
Technology
  change and, 92
  change of, 79
  selling of, 52, 54, 69
Television, 77
  sports and, 98
  trends and, 84, 85
Thinking Patterns, 49, 50
Third World, 81
Three Mile Island, 35
Time Inc., 51

Time, use of, 154
Titanic, 35, 36
Top-down approach, 11
Total systems overhaul, 9
TransAmerica/Occidental Life, 167
Transportation, industry of, 20, 132
Tregoe, Benjamin B., 181, 182
Trend Watching, 36
Turner Broadcasting Network (TBS), 84
Turner, Ted, 31, 85
TV Cable Week, 28, 51
TV Guide, 27, 28

V

Videocassettes, 48, 91, 156
　trends and, 85
Videodisks, 90, 91

W

Wall Street Journal, 179, 180
Watergate, 55, 67
Watson, Dr. (Sherlock Holmes), 161
Watson, Thomas Jr., 158
Watson, Thomas Sr., 62, 176
WGBH, 9
Wood, Robert, 33, 34
World War II, 33, 34, 45, 48, 83, 118, 126, 150, 155
Wozniak, Steve, 2, 8, 23, 124, 176
WTTW, 9